Biology Plus

Jean Martin

CAMBRIDGE
UNIVERSITY PRESS

PUBLISHED BY THE PRESS SYNDICATE OF THE UNIVERSITY OF CAMBRIDGE
The Pitt Building, Trumpington Street, Cambridge, United Kingdom

CAMBRIDGE UNIVERSITY PRESS
The Edinburgh Building, Cambridge CB2 2RU, UK
40 West 20th Street, New York, NY 10011-4211, USA
477 Williamstown Road, Port Melbourne, VIC 3207, Australia
Ruiz de Alarcón 13, 28014 Madrid, Spain
Dock House, The Waterfront, Cape Town 8001, South Africa

http://www.cambridge.org

First published 2002

Printed in the United Kingdom at the University Press, Cambridge

Typeface Stone informal   *System* QuarkXPress®

A catalogue record for this book is available from the British Library

ISBN 0 521 89236 8 paperback

Designed, edited and produced by Gecko Limited, Cambridge

Illustrations by Geoff Jones, Geoff Ward and Pete Welford

ACKNOWLEDGEMENTS
8 Hattie Young/SPL; 10 Conor Caffrey/SPL; 11l Collection CNRI/Phototake; 11r CNRI/SPL; 12t, 12b Sporting Pictures (UK) Ltd; 12c J Okwesa/TRIP; 13t David Campione/SPL; 13bl, 13br Allsport/Getty Images; 14t, 37l, 80bl, 80bc Neil Thompson; 14b Gene Cox/OSF; 15t John Adds; 15b, 48 Dr P Marazzi/SPL; 16t Educational Images/Custom Medical Stock Photo; 16b Chris Bjornberg/SPL; 18 PFT Associates; 21 Glen Cole, Enterprise Association; 27 Jim Amos/SPL; 28 D P Wilson/FLPA/Images of Nature; 29 JAL Cooke/OSF; 30 Alastair MacEwen/OSF; 31 Vaughan Fleming/SPL; 32t Claude Nuridsany & Marie Perennou/SPL; 32c Michael Sewell/OSF; 32b, 44br GI Bernard/OSF; 36 Joe Blossom/NHPA; 37r Jack Dermid/OSF; 40 D McGill/TRIP; 42t Volker Steger, Peter Arnold Inc/SPL; 42b Custom Medical Stock Photo/SPL; 44t, 70b Andrew Syred/SPL; 44ct David Scharf/SPL; 44cb Andew Syred/Microscopix; 44bl Institut Pasteur, Paris; 45t Fotomas/Topham Picturepoint; 45b BSIP, Girand/SPL; 46t, 47, 51r, 58, 63b, 67t, 68, 69c, 69b, 69t, 70c, 73t, 73b H Rogers/TRIP; 46b, 61c Mike Wyndham Picture Collection; 49 Simon Fraser/SPL; 50t Popperfoto/Reuters; 50b, 54c Mary Evans Picture Library; 51l B Seed/TRIP; 54t SPL; 54b courtesy of Professor Peter Molan & Photobank, NZ; 55t B Lake/TRIP; 55cl S Grant/TRIP; 55cr Peter Menzel/SPL; 55b N Price/TRIP; 60, 61t Andy Virco/Department of Medical Photography & Illustration, Addenbrooke's Hospital; 60c London Scientific Films/OSF; 60b Wellcome Institute Medical Picture Library; 61b Philippe Plailly/SPL; 63t Ed Reschke, Peter Arnold Inc/SPL; 64 Eye of Science/SPL; 67b GA Maclean/OSF; 70t Marcos Lopez/SPL; 72tl, tr Peter O'Toole/OSF; 72bl, 72br Anthony Blake Picture Library; 74 Maximilian Stock Ltd/SPL; 76t courtesy of Wessex Water; 76c Tommasq Guiccardini/SPL; 76b Jorgen Schytte/Still Pictures; 77 Ragendra Shaw/Panos; 80l Biophoto Associates; 80br Dr Jeremy Burgess/SPL.

Contents

■ **How to use this book**   4

■ **Moving and feeding**

1   Skeletons, support and movement   6
2   Muscles and movement   8
3   What are movable joints like?   10
4   Is exercise good for you?   12
H1   What is special about bone and cartilage?   14
H2   Joining bones and muscles   16
5   What makes fish good at swimming?   18
H3   Steering and buoyancy   20
6   What makes birds good at flying?   22
H4   Designs for flight – 1   24
H5   Designs for flight – 2   26
7   Feeding   28
H6   Mosquito bites can be dangerous   30
H7   Another piercing and sucking insect   31
H8   Some insects can't pierce skin   32
8   What's different about the way we feed?   34
9   Are all mammals' teeth the same?   36
H9   Some more adaptations to diet   38
H10   More about cellulose-digesting bacteria   40

■ **Biology in action**

I+E   1   What causes decay and disease?   42
2   How do we treat diseases?   46
3   Do antibiotics always work?   48
4   Immunity and vaccination   50
I+E   5   Vaccinations in childhood   52
I+E   6   How has the treatment of disease changed?   54
H1   More about the immune response   56
7   What happens if your kidneys fail?   58
I+E   8   Problems of kidney transplants   60
H2   More about dialysis   62
H3   Blood transfusions   63
9   Some groups of microorganisms   64
10   Using yeast to make wine and beer   66
11   Using yeast for baking   68
12   How we make yoghurt and cheese   70
13   More about making cheese   72
14   Industrial fermenters   74
I+E   H4   Biogas   76
I+E   H5   Another biofuel – ethanol   78
15   Growing microorganisms   80

■ **What you need to remember: completed passages**   82

■ **Glossary/index**   85

How to use this book

A note about the teaching sequence of modules in AQA Separate Science Biology

It is assumed in this book:

■ that the *Moving and feeding* module will be taught <u>after</u> the modules *Humans as organisms* and *Environment*

■ that the *Biology in action* module will be taught <u>after</u> the modules *Humans as organisms, Maintenance of life* and *Inheritance and selection*.

■ An introduction for students and their teachers

This book comprises two chapters:

■ *Moving and feeding*

and

■ *Biology in action*.

These chapters match the two biology modules, additional to those in Double Award Science, needed for AQA GCSE Separate Science Biology.

The material in each chapter is split into separate topics, numbered in order.

Each topic normally takes up a double-page spread, though some topics comprise just a single page and some two spreads.

There are two types of topic in each chapter:

■ topics comprising scientific ideas that <u>all</u> Separate Science Biology students are expected to know (in addition to those in Double Award Science), whether they are entered for the Foundation Tier or the Higher Tier of Separate Science Biology tests and examinations

■ topics comprising the additional scientific ideas that only candidates entered for the Higher Tier Separate Science Biology tests and examinations need to know.

Because most separate science students are entered for the Higher Tier of GCSE, the topics required by the Higher Tier only are interleaved with the topics required by all students. This provides better continuity. These Higher Tier topics are numbered H1, H2, H3 etc. both in the *Contents* and at the top of the page.

In some topics, there are ideas from your previous studies that you will be building on but which there isn't the space to explain fully again.

You will find these ideas briefly summarised like this:

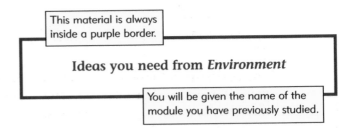

This material is always inside a purple border.

Ideas you need from *Environment*

You will be given the name of the module you have previously studied.

■ Science that all Separate Science Biology students need to know

Moving and feeding

1

| Most of the material in the book is of this type. It does not have any special border or heading. |

Skeletons, support and movement

| The answers to these questions are provided in the *Supplementary Materials*. |

Each time you are introduced to a new idea you will be asked a question.
This is so you can make sure that you really understand the ideas.

| At the end of each topic you will find a section like this. |

What you need to remember [Copy and complete using the **key words**]

You should keep your answers to these sections in a separate place. They contain all the ideas you are expected to remember and understand in tests and examinations. So they are very useful for revision.

It is very important that these summaries are correct, so you should always check your summaries against those provided on pages 82–84 of this book.

■ Science that only Higher Tier students need to know

Moving and feeding

H2 For Higher Tier students only
Joining bones and muscles

| There will be a heading like this. |

| This material is always inside a brown border. |

You will find questions in the text. Your answers to these questions will provide you with a summary of the additional ideas that you are expected to remember and understand for Higher Tier tests and examinations. You should keep them with your 'What you need to remember' summaries so you can use them for revision.

| Because the answers to these questions are a summary of what is on the extension pages, no further answers are provided. |

| At the end of each topic you will find a section like this. |

Using your knowledge

The questions in these sections are like many of the questions you will meet in Higher Tier tests and examinations. You have to use ideas from the topic to explain something new. You are <u>not</u> expected to remember the answers to these questions.

| Answers to these questions are provided in the *Supplementary Materials*. |

■ A note about practical work

Practical work, where you observe things and find out things for yourself, is an important part of Science. You will often see things in this book which you have yourself seen or done, but detailed instructions for practical work are not included. These will be provided separately by your teacher.

| The *Supplementary Materials* contain many suggestions for practical activities. |

■ A note about *Ideas and evidence*

All GCSE Science specifications must now assess candidates' understanding of what the National Curriculum calls *Ideas and evidence*. Those parts of this book which deal with this aspect of Science are indicated, on the *Contents* page, like this:

I+E 1 What causes decay and disease? _____ 36

Skeletons, support and movement

We call skeletons that are inside the body **internal** skeletons. Humans, other mammals, birds, reptiles, amphibians and fish all have internal skeletons. Scientists put all these animals together in a group called vertebrates.

One of the important jobs of your skeleton is to enable you to move about. It does this by giving your muscles something firm and rigid to pull on. Most animals have to move about to find food.

1 Write down <u>three</u> important jobs that your skeleton does.

How does your skeleton do its jobs?

Your skeleton is made of lots of bones. To support your body, each bone needs to be rigid, and all the bones in your skeleton need to be joined together firmly. To help you **move** around, some of these bones must also be able to move. Your skeleton can support your body <u>and</u> enable you to move about because of the way your bones are joined together. The places where bones meet are called joints. Bones can move at some joints, but not at others.

2 There is no movement between the bones in your skull. Why do you think this is?

3 Look at the diagram. Write down <u>two</u> parts of your skeleton where bones need to move at joints.

> **What use is a skeleton?**
> - It protects some of the soft parts of your body.
> - It supports your body.
> - It gives muscles something to pull on. So it helps you to move about.

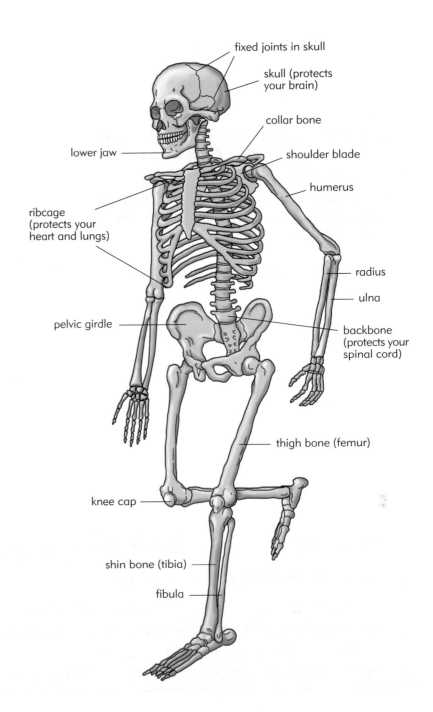

fixed joints in skull
skull (protects your brain)
collar bone
lower jaw
shoulder blade
humerus
ribcage (protects your heart and lungs)
radius
ulna
pelvic girdle
backbone (protects your spinal cord)
thigh bone (femur)
knee cap
shin bone (tibia)
fibula

How do your muscles help?

The flesh that covers your bones is made of muscles.
Muscles are attached to bones. They pull on the bones to
move parts of your body.

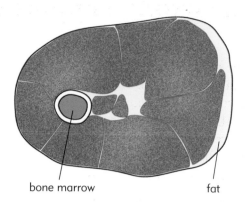

bone marrow   fat

4 Copy the drawing of the section of a leg.
  Label the bone and muscles.
  Add a layer of skin on the outside.

Muscles that move bones work in pairs. When one
contracts, the other relaxes. We call them **antagonistic**
pairs because they work against each other.

When a muscle contracts it gets shorter and fatter,
so it pulls on the bone. The other muscle of the pair
relaxes to let the bone move.

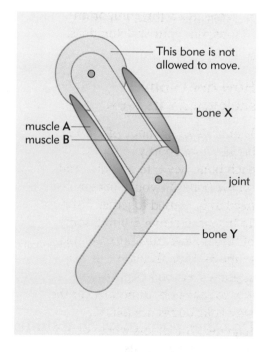

5 Look at the diagram. When muscle **A** contracts, what
  happens to:

  (a) muscle **B**?

  (b) bone **Y**?

What you need to remember [Copy and complete using the **key words**]

Skeletons, support and movement

Vertebrates have _____ skeletons made of lots of bones.
Bones are the rigid framework that gives you support and lets you _____.
Muscles are attached to bones in _____ pairs.
When one muscle of a pair contracts, the other _____.

Muscles and movement

An example of an antagonistic pair of muscles is the pair of muscles you use to bend and straighten your arm at the elbow.

1 Look at the pictures. Write down the muscle that contracts to:

  (a) bend the arm

  (b) straighten the arm.

Contracted muscles are short and fat, so they bulge.

When your biceps **contracts**, your triceps **relaxes**. The triceps gets longer and thinner to <u>let</u> the lower arm bones move. So it is only the **contracting** muscle of a pair that actually moves the bone.

2 Describe the shape of a:

  (a) contracted muscle

  (b) relaxed muscle.

3 What do we mean when we call the biceps and triceps muscles an antagonistic pair?

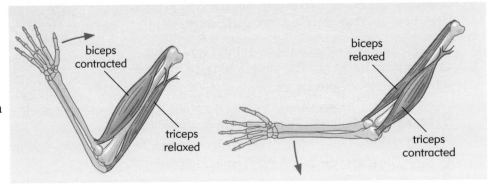

The biceps and triceps work against each other, so we call them an antagonistic pair.

■ Do other parts move in a similar way?

The diagram shows the bones and a few of the muscles in a human leg.

4 Look at the diagram, then copy and complete the sentences:
Muscles _____ and _____ are an antagonistic pair.
When muscle _____ contracts, muscle _____ relaxes.
Muscle _____ is the one doing the work.

5 Which muscle contracts to lift the leg forwards at the hip joint?

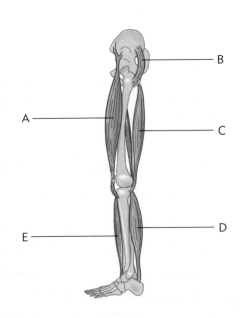

◼ Which muscles are being used?

On long flights in a plane, people can't move about very much. As a result, a few people develop blood clots in their legs.

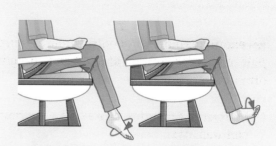

The pictures show John doing some exercises to prevent this. Use the diagram on page 8 to help you to answer the questions.

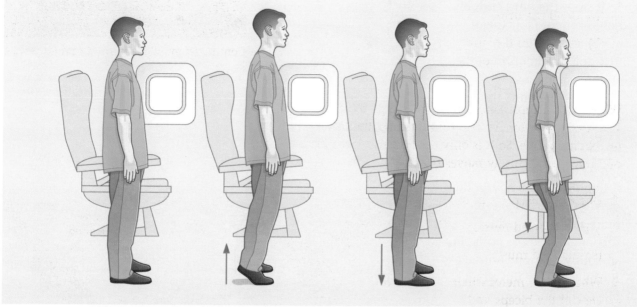

6 (a) Which muscle does John contract to point his toes?

   (b) Which muscle does he relax?

   (c) Which of the <u>two</u> muscles is doing the work?

7 Which muscle does he contract to bend his foot back up?

8 At the end of the second exercise, muscles **C** and **E** are contracted. Describe what happens to muscles **A** to **E** as John stands up straight again.

What you need to remember [Copy and complete using the **key words**]

Muscles and movement

When one muscle of an antagonistic pair _____, the other muscle _____.
It is only the _____ muscle that does the work to make a bone move.

[When you are given information, you need to be able to describe the effects of muscles and bones on movement.]

What are movable joints like?

Bone is rigid and strong.
In movable joints, the ends
of the bones are covered with
cartilage.
Cartilage is a smoother and
softer tissue than bone.
So it stops the hard ends of
bones rubbing together.

1 Copy the diagram of the
thigh bone.
Colour the parts that
have a covering of
cartilage.

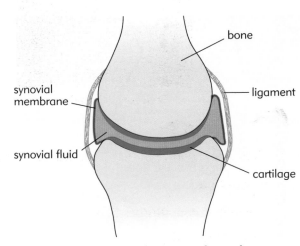

This part fits into the
socket in the pelvic girdle.

These parts move against
the lower leg bones.

Human thigh bone.

A liquid called **synovial** fluid
makes the cartilage even
more slippery. It reduces
friction, letting the parts slip
smoothly over one another.
It acts a bit like the oil on a
bicycle chain.

2 Copy and complete
the table:

Part of the joint	What it does
cartilage	
synovial membrane	
synovial fluid	

bone

synovial
membrane

synovial fluid

ligament

cartilage

A synovial joint. The synovial membrane
secretes synovial fluid.

3 Andrea is hoping to have
her hip joint replaced
with an artificial one.
What difference will a
new hip make to her life?

Arthritis has damaged
the cartilage in Andrea's
hip joint and made
it rough. She finds
walking difficult
and painful.

What keeps bones in place?

Strong fibrous bands hold bones together. We call them **ligaments**. In normal use, they stretch just enough to let the bones move at joints. Very occasionally a bone slips out of place. When this happens, we say that a bone has become dislocated. It is very painful.

4 Ligaments stretch only very slightly. Why is this?

5 Look at the X-rays. Describe the difference between the normal and the dislocated shoulder.

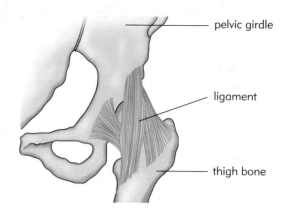

Ligaments hold bones together.

pelvic girdle

ligament

thigh bone

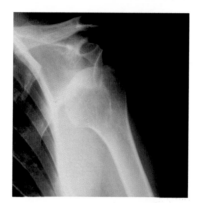

Dislocated shoulder.

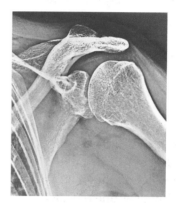

Normal shoulder.

6 Copy the diagram of the hip joint. Add these labels:

- ligament
- synovial membrane
- synovial fluid
- bone
- cartilage.

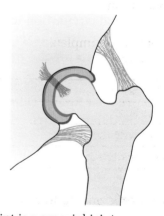

The hip joint is a synovial joint.

What you need to remember [Copy and complete using the **key words**]

What are movable joints like?

Strong fibres called _____ hold the bones together at joints.
Movable joints such as your knee move easily because:

- the ends of the bones are covered in smooth _____ to stop the bones rubbing together
- a membrane secretes oily _____ fluid to make the cartilage slippery.

4

Is exercise good for you?

> ### Ideas you need from *Humans as organisms*
> - Muscle tissue contains fibres that contract.
> - To contract, they use energy released in respiration.

Karen works out to keep her muscle fibres slightly tensed. We say that she has good muscle tone.

Some people's jobs or lifestyles mean that they get plenty of exercise. This keeps them in good condition. What this means is that circulation of blood to their heart, lungs and muscles works efficiently.

When you exercise, your heart beats faster and you breathe faster and more deeply. In the short term, this means that your muscles:

- obtain glucose and **oxygen** at a faster rate
- get rid of **carbon dioxide** and heat at a faster rate.

1 When you exercise, why do your muscles need:

   (a) more glucose and oxygen?

   (b) to get rid of heat?

In the long term, regular exercise helps to maintain an efficient blood **circulation** through your heart, lungs and muscles. Sports trainers call this maintaining your aerobic fitness. It can also make you feel good.

Sarah is trying to increase her stamina.
She wants to run without feeling stiff and sore afterwards.

Some people exercise to develop their muscles as well as to improve their fitness. Different sorts of exercise affect muscles in different ways.

2 Look at the photographs. Then copy and complete the table.

Type of exercise	How does it help your muscles?
running	
weight training	
trim and tone class	

3 Nick also runs three times a week.
Why do you think he does this?

Nick is a javelin thrower. He also does weight training to make his muscles **stronger**.

Exercise also helps to keep your **joints** working smoothly. If you don't exercise you become less flexible and your joints become stiff.

■ Can exercise cause problems?

Look at the picture. Clare's joints are very flexible and her ligaments stretch easily enough for her to do this. It wouldn't be wise to try this yourself. You need to go to a class. If you don't build up to it in the right way, you can damage your joints or pull a muscle. It is also important to learn the correct way to do the other exercises shown on these pages.

Yoga helps Clare to stay supple and flexible.

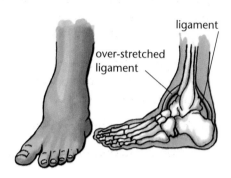

4 When we damage ligaments and other tissues in a joint, what do we say we have done?

5 Dee tells you that she wants to learn yoga. To be safe, what should she do? Explain your answer.

Peter sprained his ankle. He overstretched the ligaments so the joint is swollen and painful. It will take weeks or months to recover fully.

Many runners damage their ankles or knees as a result of poor running style.
Other people damage their backs using weights. Sudden jerky movements, turns and falls can lead to pulled muscles, damaged ligaments and broken bones. Bones can also be dislocated or forced out of joints.

6 Why do athletes do warm-ups and stretches?

Doing warm-ups and stretches at the start of exercise sessions reduces the risk of pulled muscles and damaged joints.

What you need to remember [Copy and complete using the **key words**]

Is exercise good for you?

When you exercise:
- glucose and _____ are supplied to your muscles at a faster rate
- heat and _____ _____ are removed from your muscles at a faster rate.

Regular exercise:
- keeps the _____ of the blood to the heart, lungs and muscles working efficiently
- keeps muscles toned
- makes muscles _____ and able to work for longer
- keeps _____ working smoothly.

But, you need to avoid sudden wrenches that can cause sprains and dislocations.

H1 For Higher Tier students only

What is special about bone and cartilage?

What is bone tissue like?

Bone tissue contains living cells and proteins.
You can boil bones to extract a protein called gelatine.
To give support, bones need to be stiff. So bone tissue is hardened by a chemical called calcium phosphate.
The chemical itself is brittle, but the proteins make the bone less brittle and less likely to break.

<table>
<tr><td colspan="2">REMEMBER</td></tr>
<tr><td>■ A bone is an organ.</td></tr>
<tr><td>■ It is made of bone tissue, cartilage and other tissues.</td></tr>
</table>

1 Write down <u>three</u> things that bone tissue contains.

2 Look at the photograph.
   Explain why this chicken bone bends.

3 Look at the table. Which <u>one</u> of these properties makes bone a good material for support?

Property of bone	What this means
hard	not easily marked by scratching
stiff	not easily deformed by bending
not brittle	not easily broken by hitting it
strong	not easily broken by stretching or compressing

This chicken bone was soaked in acid. The acid removed the calcium phosphate. Now the bone bends.

Because bone is stiff and strong, you cannot:

■ compress it

■ stretch it

■ bend it.

It takes quite a lot of force to break a bone. But the living cells in bone tissue can repair a broken bone.

4 Write down <u>three</u> forces that bones resist.

5 Think of a reason why bones have a blood supply.

6 What is the part of the bone between the cells made from?

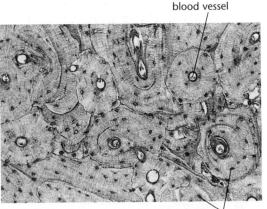

blood vessel

Bone tissue.

bone cells

What is cartilage tissue like?

Like bone, cartilage contains cells. But it doesn't contain calcium phosphate, so it is not rigid. However, it is strong enough to support soft tissues. Because it can be compressed slightly, it is also useful as a shock absorber.

You can feel cartilage in the firmer parts of your ears and nose. The cartilage supports them without making them rigid.

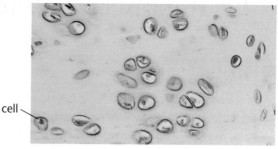

cell

Cartilage gives a smooth surface to bones at joints.

7 Some properties of cartilage are that it:

■ is smooth

■ is strong, but not rigid

■ can be compressed slightly

■ has very little elasticity.

Which properties are important in cartilage:

(a) in your nose?

(b) between the bones in your spine?

(c) at the ends of bones in your limbs?

Explain your answers.

Section through a nose

one of the small bones of your spine

ligament

cartilage

☐ bone

■ cartilage

☐ flesh (skin, muscle and fat)

Using your knowledge

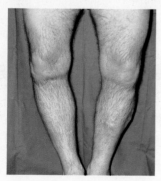

Humans need vitamin D to help them to absorb calcium from their food. Alf didn't get enough vitamin D so he developed rickets.

1 (a) Alf's leg bones bent as he grew. Explain this as fully as you can.

(b) Later, Alf had plenty of calcium and vitamin D. His bones are now rigid but not straight. Why is this?

2 Some people get a condition called osteoporosis. Their bones start to lose calcium phosphate. This can happen to anyone at any age. It is most common in older women.
Try to explain the following facts.
As osteoporosis gets worse, people:

(a) break bones more easily

(b) become shorter in height

(c) float more easily in water.

[You will not be expected to give details of the microscopic structure of the tissues on this spread.]

H2 For Higher Tier students only

Joining bones and muscles

More about ligaments

Ligaments are made of long fibres that are strong and not easily broken by stretching. We say that they have tensile strength. They stretch so little that we say they have very little elasticity. In normal use, they stretch just enough to let bones move at joints.

1 (a) Explain the meaning of tensile strength and elasticity.

(b) Why do ligaments need tensile strength and some elasticity?

2 Describe what ligament tissue looks like under a microscope.

It is important that ligaments don't let bones move out of place. When this does happen, we say that a bone has become dislocated.

3 Look at the X-ray.

(a) What injury does it show?

(b) Why isn't this a common injury?

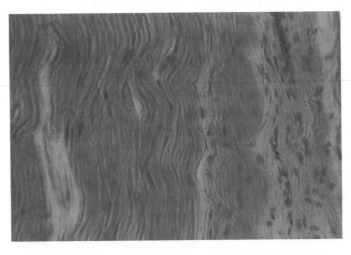

It is hard to break a bundle of fibres like these by pulling on them.

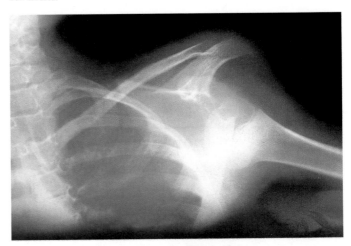

Ben dislocated his shoulder playing rugby.

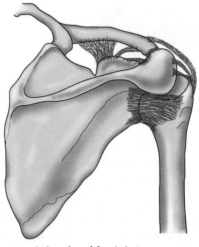

Ligaments around the shoulder joint.

What joins muscles to bones?

Muscles have one or more tendons at each end. One end of each tendon is attached to the muscle; the other is fixed firmly to a bone.

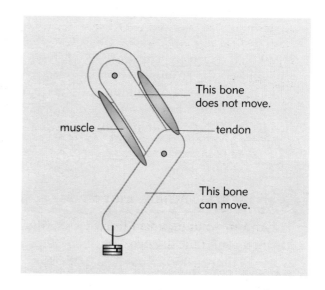

muscle

tendon

4 Look at the model. When the muscle contracts, it gets shorter.
What happens if:

(a) the tendons are made of elastic?

(b) the tendons are inelastic?

This bone does not move.

muscle — — tendon

This bone can move.

Muscles contract to move bones.
So the tissue that joins a muscle to a bone should not stretch easily.
We say that it should have little elasticity.
It also needs to have tensile strength.
It is rare for a tendon to break.

5 Why does tendon tissue have:

(a) little elasticity?

(b) tensile strength?

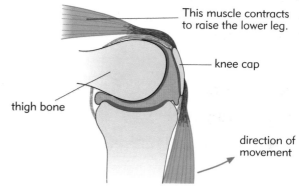

This muscle contracts to raise the lower leg.

knee cap

thigh bone

direction of movement

When a muscle contracts, tendons don't stretch – so the muscle pulls on the bones.

Using your knowledge

1 Ben dislocated his shoulder. The doctor warned him that it could happen more easily another time. Why do you think this is?

2 Cherie snapped her Achilles tendon in a skiing accident. It was very painful.
The doctor stitched it together and put her foot in plaster so that she could not move it. What movement was Cherie unable to make when her Achilles tendon broke? Explain your answer.

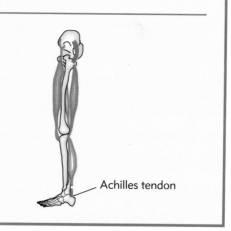

Achilles tendon

What makes fish good at swimming?

If you are a swimmer, you will know that you can move on land faster and more easily than you can move through water. This is because water is denser than air. It offers more resistance. We say that it causes more drag.

Because of the way they dart about, fish often look as though they are swimming fast. Goldfish swim at about 4 km/h and a speeding salmon at about four times that speed. The fastest fish is probably a sailfish. It can swim at 110 km/h. A few human swimmers can reach 8 km/h for a short time.

■ A shape that makes movement easier

Fish are better at moving through water than we are. One reason is that their **streamlined** shape reduces water resistance and creates less drag.

1 What do we mean by water resistance?

2 Why is it more difficult to move through water than through air?

3 Write down <u>one</u> adaptation of fish that helps them overcome water resistance.

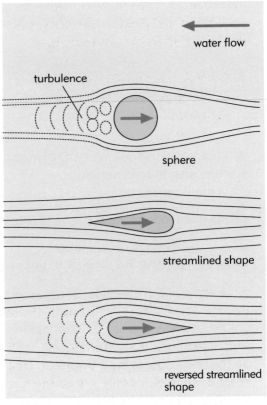

Some shapes create less turbulence than others as they move through water. Turbulence causes drag.

■ Muscles that produce movement

Fish are vertebrates, so they have a **backbone**. Like yours, a fish's backbone is made of lots of bones and the **muscles** are arranged along either side.

The swimming muscles of a fish make up most of the weight of its body. They are the part of the fish that people eat.

4 Copy and complete the sentence.

In a fish, there is a zig-zag arrangement of _____ along both sides of the _____.

Like other muscles, the fish's muscles work in pairs. When a muscle on one side of the fish contracts, the muscle on the other side relaxes. As contractions pass along the length of the body, they produce a **wave-like** movement.

5 Copy the diagram of the fish. Write either C or R in the boxes on your copy.

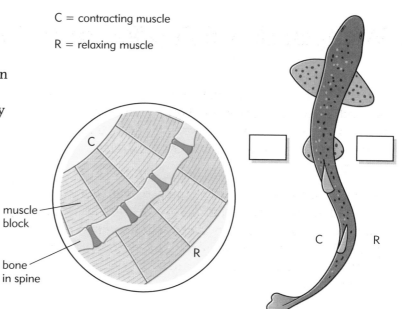

C = contracting muscle

R = relaxing muscle

muscle block

bone in spine

How a fish pushes itself forward

As the wave of contractions passes along the fish, the **tail fin** pushes on the water. The large surface area of the tail fin makes the push more effective. It's a bit like the effect that <u>you</u> get from wearing flippers when you swim. A pushing force is called a thrust. The fish pushes on the water first on one side, then the other. The effect of this is a backward thrust on the water. This moves the fish forwards.

6 Look at diagrams 1 and 3 then write down the direction of:

(a) the thrust of the tail on the water

(b) the resultant thrusts on the fish

(c) the movement of the fish.

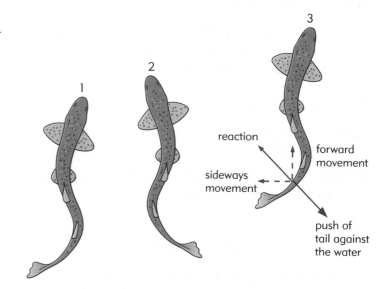

reaction

sideways movement

forward movement

push of tail against the water

The reaction force of the water on the tail fin can be split into two parts:

↑ this part pushes the fish forwards
←-- this part pushes the fish sideways.

What you need to remember [Copy and complete using the **key words**]

What makes fish good at swimming?

Fish are adapted for moving in water.

They have a _____ shape to reduce water resistance.

There is a zig-zag arrangement of _____ on either side of the _____. As contractions of these muscles pass along the body, they produce a _____-_____ movement.

The _____ _____ has a large surface area. This fin is pushed backwards against the water, so the fish moves forwards.

H3 For Higher Tier students only
Steering and buoyancy

Fish have single fins and paired fins.

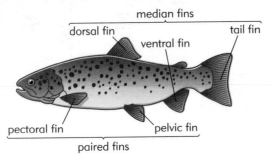

The single, or median, fins increase the vertical surface area of the fish. They help to keep it upright and to resist side-to-side movements. They work a bit like the centreboard of a sailing dinghy.

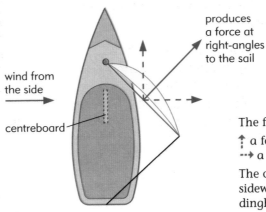

The force on the sail has

↑ a forward part, and
┈➤ a sideways part.

The centreboard resists the sideways thrust and so the dinghy only moves forwards.

1 Copy the top diagram of the fish. Shade the tail fin, the paired fins and the median fins in different colours. Add a key for the colours.

2 Label your diagram to show:

    (a) the fins that increase the vertical surface area of the fish

    (b) the fin that pushes on the water to make the fish move forwards.

3 Explain how the median fins help to:

    (a) keep the fish upright

    (b) reduce sideways movement.

The other fins have different jobs, such as steering and braking.

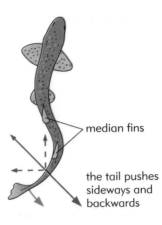

The reaction force of the water on the fish's tail has

↑ a forward part, and
◂┈ a sideways part.

But the median fins resist sideways movement, so the fish only moves forwards.

The median fins also reduce rolling and keep the fish upright.

How a fish steers

The paired fins control the up and down movements of the fish. They also act as brakes and enable the fish to move backwards.

4 Which directions of movement do the paired fins control?

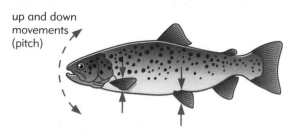

Paired fins help to resist up and down movements. But the fish can move up or down by slanting these fins.

What stops fish sinking?

Some fish sink when they stop swimming. Sharks are like this. They can rest only on the bottom of the sea. This is because their bodies are denser than seawater.

Other fish have swim bladders filled with gas. These lower the density of the fish. The more gas there is in the swim bladder, the higher the fish floats in the water. A fish can change the depth at which it floats in the water by altering the amount of gas in its swim bladder.

5 (a) Describe exactly where a fish's swim bladder is.

  (b) Explain how it provides buoyancy.

6 What part of a sailing dinghy is equivalent to a swim bladder?

The buoyancy bags are full of air, so they will help to keep this dinghy afloat if it capsizes.

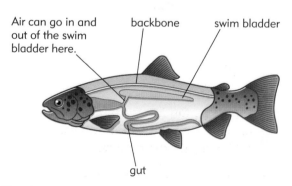

This fish can let air in and out of its swim bladder, so it can rest at different depths. A swim bladder is a bit like a built-in buoyancy bag.

Using your knowledge

1 Some fish, such as herring, let air in and out of their swim bladders through their mouths. In others, such as the lantern fish, the swim bladder has no opening. Gases enter and leave the bladder via the blood.

Which of these fish is likely to change the depth at which it rests more quickly? Explain your answer.

What makes birds good at flying?

■ Birds have a small mass for their size

Birds are vertebrates, so they have internal skeletons made of bone. Their skeletons are specialised for flight. Their limb bones are a bit like tubes of strong bone, **honey-combed** inside with lots of air spaces. The air spaces make them lighter than the bones of other vertebrates. This makes it easier for birds to fly.

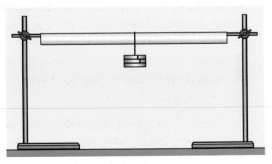

This card is rolled into a cylinder.

1   Look at the pictures.
    Which structure is the stronger?

2   (a) What is the advantage to a bird of having
         light bones?

    (b) Why must the bones also be strong?

3   Explain how a bird's bones can be both light
    and strong.

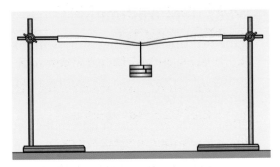

This is the same type and amount of card rolled up tightly.

Wings pushing down on the air help to give a bird lift. So a bird needs wings with a large surface area. Flight feathers give the wings this large **surface area** without adding so much mass that the bird cannot fly.

4   A bird's wings have a large surface area.
    Why is this necessary?

5   Feathers are strong and light for their size.
    Explain why this is important.

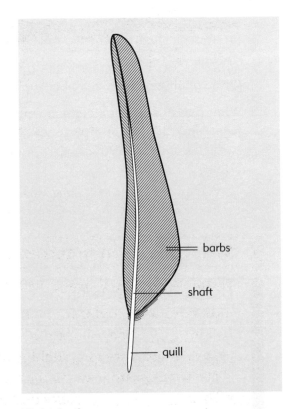

barbs

shaft

quill

Flight feather.

A bird's shape also helps it to fly

Like a fish, a bird has a **streamlined** body shape to reduce drag or **air resistance**. The better the streamlining, the less effort the bird has to use to move forwards.

6 Which bird, A or B, has the better body shape for reducing air resistance?

7 Suppose both birds have the same mass and fly at the same speed. Which one, A or B, uses the most energy to fly for 1 kilometre?

8 Look at the diagram below. Put the following sentences in the correct order.

When a bird flies:

- the muscles labelled A contract
- the wings push down on the air
- the bird's body is lifted
- the wings are pulled down
- air resistance causes upthrust.

bird A

bird B

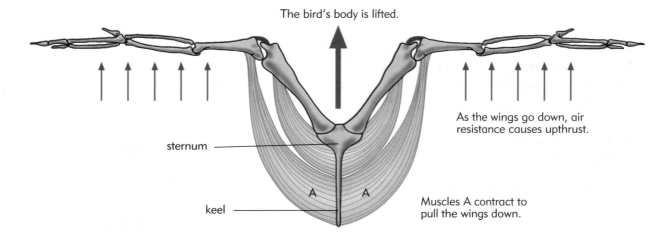

The bird's body is lifted.

As the wings go down, air resistance causes upthrust.

sternum

keel

Muscles A contract to pull the wings down.

What you need to remember [Copy and complete using the **key words**]

What makes birds good at flying?

Most birds are adapted for flight.

- Their _____ body shape reduces drag or _____ _____.
- Their wings have long flight feathers so their _____ _____ is large.
  The wings push down on the air to lift the bird up.
- Their _____- _____ bones and their feathers are strong, but light in mass.

H4 For Higher Tier students only
Designs for flight – 1

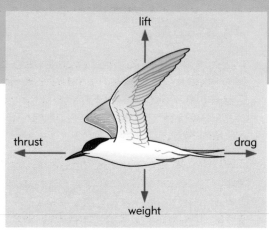

Forces acting on a bird in flight.

Shape

A bird's streamlined shape helps it to overcome the air resistance or drag that makes it harder to move forwards. But air resistance is important to produce the upthrust on the wings that causes lift.

The shape of the cross-section of a wing is important for giving a bird lift:

- The airflow over the top of the wing is faster than the flow under the wing.

- So the pressure below the wing is higher.

- The higher pressure or upthrust gives the bird lift.

1 Which <u>two</u> forces resist take-off and flight?

2 (a) Draw an aerofoil shape.

  (b) Describe how this shape produces lift.

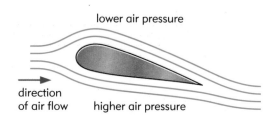

This shape is called an aerofoil.

Flight feathers

Notice the overlapping arrangement of flight feathers.
Different birds fly in different ways.
In flapping flight the bird gains:

- lift from the secondary feathers

- forward thrust by turning its wrist on the downbeat to push the primary feathers back against the air.

3 A bird's wing has primary and secondary feathers.
Describe the differences in:

 (a) their positions

 (b) their jobs.

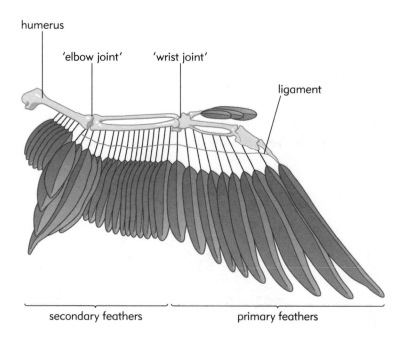

Arrangement of wing bones and flight feathers.

The way that the feathers overlap also helps with lift. Air cannot pass between the feathers as the wing goes down, but it can as the wing goes up. So the wing pushes on the air much more on the downbeat than on the upbeat.

Feathers also help to provide the smooth surface and the tapering shape of the wings.

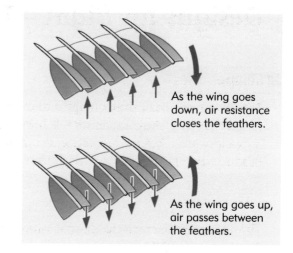

As the wing goes down, air resistance closes the feathers.

As the wing goes up, air passes between the feathers.

4 (a) Describe the difference between the position of the flight feathers on the downbeat and the upbeat.

  (b) Explain why this difference is important.

5 Look at the diagram, then copy and complete the table.

Flight feathers should be	Adaptation for this
light	
strong	
smooth and flat	

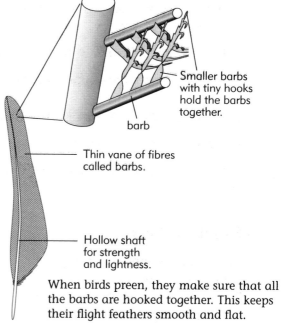

Smaller barbs with tiny hooks hold the barbs together.

barb

Thin vane of fibres called barbs.

Hollow shaft for strength and lightness.

6 Birds must keep their feathers in good condition. Explain how they do this.

When birds preen, they make sure that all the barbs are hooked together. This keeps their flight feathers smooth and flat.

Using your knowledge

1 Look at the two wing feathers. Which one is from a flightless bird? Explain your answer as fully as you can.

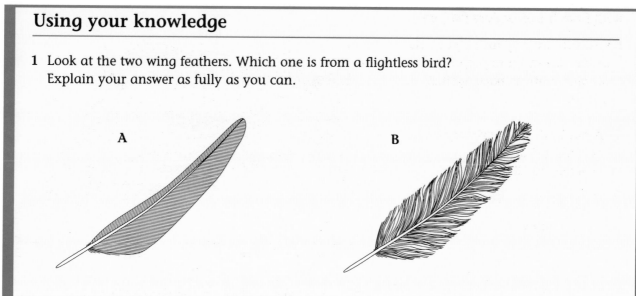

A

B

H5 For Higher Tier students only

Designs for flight – 2

■ Wing bones

The arrangement of bones in your limbs is similar to that in other vertebrates.

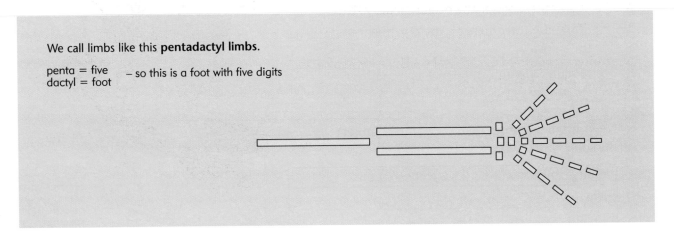

We call limbs like this **pentadactyl limbs**.

penta = five
dactyl = foot

– so this is a foot with five digits

A bird's wing evolved from a pentadactyl limb. The number of digits and wrist bones became smaller to form a more tapering structure.

1 What is a pentadactyl limb?

2 How many bones form:

(a) the upper limb?

(b) the lower limb?

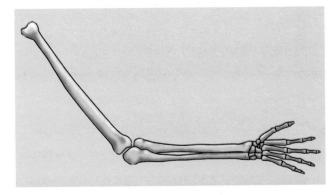

Human arm bones.

3 In a bird, the pentadactyl limb evolved into a longer, thinner structure. Write down the <u>two</u> groups of bones involved in these changes.

4 Describe the differences between the bones in a bird's wing and a human arm.

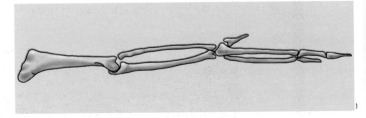

Bird wing bones.
Note: The wing and arm bones are drawn to different scales.

Sternum

Flying takes lots of effort so birds need huge flight muscles. One end of these muscles is attached to the sternum (breastbone), on an extension called the keel.

The keel provides:

■ a rigid framework

■ a large surface area for the attachment of these large muscles.

5 Explain the presence of a keel on the sternum as an adaptation for flight.

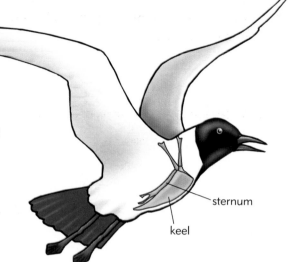

sternum

keel

Using your knowledge

1 The pictures show the skeleton of an animal that lived 150 million years ago. It had feathers and a lot of other features of birds.

   (a) Write down <u>two</u> features of this skeleton which are like that of a bird, and <u>two</u> features that are different.

   (b) Most scientists think that it did not have muscles that were big enough for flying. Write down <u>one</u> feature of the skeleton that supports this idea.

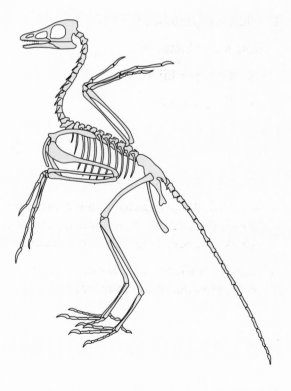

Reconstructions of skeletons are based on fossils – like this one of *Archaeopteryx*.

7

Feeding

Ideas you need from *Environment*

■ Animals eat plants or other animals. Some eat animal and plant wastes and remains.

■ Each kind of animal is adapted to feeding on particular types of food in its own way.

How mussels feed

The mussels that you can find on rocky seashores or at the fishmongers are only one of nearly a million different species of invertebrates.
Invertebrates are animals that don't have backbones.

Mussels feed on microscopic plants and animals called **plankton** that live in seawater.
Mussel **gills** are a bit like sieves.
They filter plankton from the water.

Mussels do not move about. They spend their lives fixed to rock by strong threads.

1 Mussels can feed only when the tide is in, that is, when they are under water.
Why is this?

The cells of mussel gills are covered with tiny beating hairs called **cilia**. Some of the cilia make a **current** of water flow through the body. Others move the plankton **trapped** on the gills towards the mouth.

2 (a) What are cilia?

(b) Explain how mussels use cilia to feed.

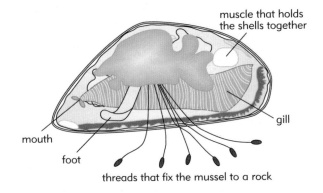

A mussel filters about 4.5 litres of water a day.

3 Make a copy of the diagram to show the water currents.

Label the arrow that shows water going into the mussel 'water containing plankton'.

Label the arrow leaving the mussel 'water without plankton'.

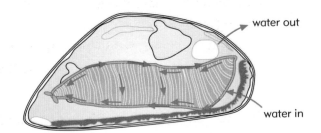

How mosquitoes feed

Mosquitoes are also invertebrates. Only the adult females feed on **blood**. They need a blood meal before they can lay their eggs. We talk about mosquito 'bites', but when a mosquito 'bites' you, it actually pierces your **skin** with its proboscis. Then it sucks up the blood from a capillary through a tube that is a bit like a drinking straw.

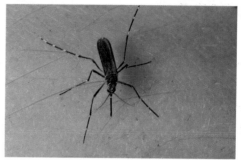

A mosquito ready to feed. Mosquitoes are most active in the evening.

4 Look at the photograph and diagrams. Describe the mosquito's mouthparts.

One problem of feeding on blood is that blood clots. A clot can block a thin proboscis. So a mosquito makes special **saliva** that prevents clotting. It secretes this saliva into the capillary first. Then it uses muscles in its throat as a pump to draw up the blood.

5 Write down <u>three</u> adaptations of mosquitoes for feeding on blood.

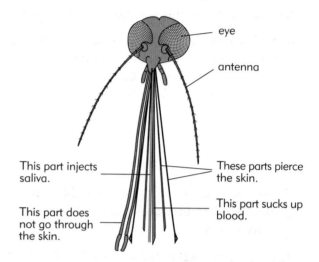

eye

antenna

This part injects saliva.

These parts pierce the skin.

This part does not go through the skin.

This part sucks up blood.

A mosquito's jaws (**proboscis**) are a bit like hypodermic needles. (The jaws have been spread out to make them clearer. Usually they are arranged as shown in the section.)

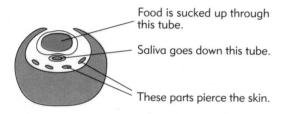

Food is sucked up through this tube.

Saliva goes down this tube.

These parts pierce the skin.

A section through a mosquito's feeding tube.

What you need to remember [Copy and complete using the **key words**]

Feeding

Mussels feed by using their _____ to trap _____.
Beating hairs called _____:
- draw a _____ of water containing the plankton through the body
- move the _____ plankton towards the mouth.

A mosquito feeds on _____.
- It has a sharp, needle-like _____ to pierce the _____ and go into a capillary.
- It secretes _____ into the blood to stop it clotting.
- It uses muscles in its throat to suck up the _____.

H6 For Higher Tier students only

Mosquito bites can be dangerous

Mosquito saliva sometimes contains microorganisms that cause disease. They can be injected into the blood. One example is the **malaria** parasite. **Parasites** live and feed on other living organisms. Some live inside the body and others on the surface.

The malaria parasite spends part of its lifecycle in the salivary glands of a mosquito called *Anopheles*. It spends the other part in human blood. It has only one cell. It is so small that it feeds and reproduces inside human red blood cells.

1 (a) What is a parasite?

 (b) Where does the malaria parasite live? Answer this as fully as you can.

2 Look at the diagram. Describe how the malaria parasite is spread from one person to another.

While the parasites are feeding and reproducing inside the blood cells, a malaria patient feels well. Then the red cells burst and release parasites and toxins into the blood. The parasites go into new blood cells. The patient develops a severe fever. The patient is first cold, then hot, then sweaty and may die. If not, the whole cycle repeats itself. Up to $2\frac{1}{2}$ million people die from malaria every year.

3 What causes the fever in malaria patients?

> ## REMEMBER
>
> When a mosquito feeds on you, it secretes saliva into your blood.

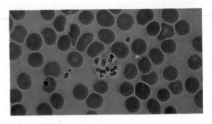

Parasites reproduce in the stomach wall then move to the salivary glands.

The mosquito injects parasites into the blood in saliva.

The mosquito sucks up blood and becomes infected with malaria parasites.

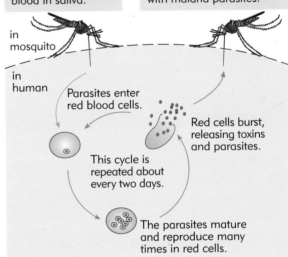

in mosquito

in human

Parasites enter red blood cells.

Red cells burst, releasing toxins and parasites.

This cycle is repeated about every two days.

The parasites mature and reproduce many times in red cells.

Life cycle of the malaria parasite.

Using your knowledge

1 Health advice for travellers going to countries where *Anopheles* mosquitoes live is:

 ■ Take anti-malaria tablets for a week before you go, while you are there, and for a month after you return home. These tablets kill the parasites <u>outside</u> the blood cells.
 ■ Use an insect repellent on your skin.
 ■ Cover your arms and legs during the evening.
 ■ Sleep under a mosquito net treated with insecticide.
 Explain the advice as fully as you can.

 [Note: An <u>insect repellent</u> is a substance that insects avoid.
 An <u>insecticide</u> kills insects.]

H7 For Higher Tier students only
Another piercing and sucking insect

Aphids are a group of insects that include greenfly and blackfly. They feed on plant sap in much the same way as mosquitoes feed on blood. So, their mouthparts are very similar to those of mosquitoes. They are adapted for piercing plant tissues, then sucking sap from a vein.

1 List the adaptations of an aphid for feeding on plant sap.

2 Write down <u>two</u> reasons why gardeners try to get rid of aphids from their plants.

Aphids feeding on a lupin. When lots of aphids feed on a plant, they can weaken it. They can also infect it with viruses carried from other plants.

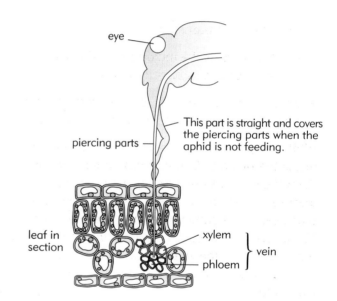

eye

piercing parts

This part is straight and covers the piercing parts when the aphid is not feeding.

leaf in section

xylem
phloem
} vein

Using your knowledge

1 (a) Which part, A to D, does not pierce skin?
   What happens to it when the insect feeds?

   (b) Saliva goes down tube A.
   What happens in tube B?

   (c) In a feeding insect, where is the very tip of (i) C, and (ii) D?

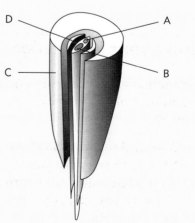

D   A

C   B

Tip of the mouthparts of a piercing and sucking insect.

31

H8 For Higher Tier students only

Some insects can't pierce skin

Some other insects also feed by sucking fluids into their mouths. But they don't have parts for piercing skin like those of aphids and mosquitoes.
They feed on fluids that are exposed, or foods that they have been either partly digested or dissolved.

Butterflies

A butterfly's mouthparts are not rigid, so its **proboscis** can coil up under its head.
When it feeds, it uncoils its proboscis and sucks sugary nectar from flowers.
It drinks water in the same way.

1 What does a butterfly mainly feed on?

2 Why do we call a butterfly a sucking insect, not a piercing and sucking insect?

A butterfly's proboscis is like a coiled-up drinking straw.

Sometimes a butterfly sucks urine, tears or sweat to get the salt.

Houseflies

You have probably seen houseflies feeding on meat, sugar and all sorts of other foods. But they can only take in fluids. So they have to make their food into a fluid. First they secrete saliva onto the food. This dissolves some substances, and digests and dissolves others. Then they can suck them up.

3 Look at the diagram, then explain the jobs of:

(a) the salivary gland

(b) the channels in the end of the proboscis

(c) the oesophagus

(d) the muscles.

4 Copy and complete the table.

Type of feeding	Example of insect
piercing and sucking	(i) _____
	(ii) _____
sucking	(i) _____
	(ii) _____

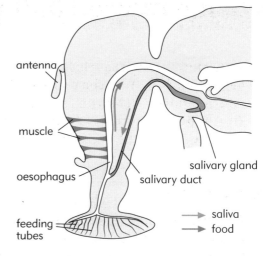

A housefly's proboscis has lots of tiny tubes for sucking up fluids from a large area.

Using your knowledge

1 Look at the drawings.
Which insect feeds by:

- piercing and sucking?
- sucking fluids?
- neither piercing nor sucking?

Give reasons for your answers.

2 Explain how a housefly can transfer bacteria from one food to another as it feeds.

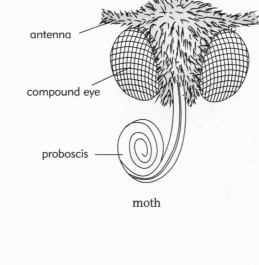

moth

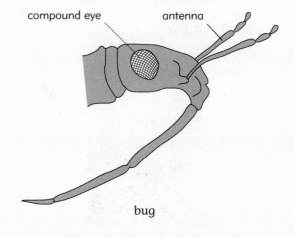

bug

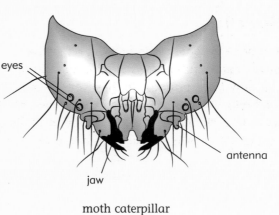

moth caterpillar

8

What's different about the way we feed?

Humans and other mammals can eat a mixture of solids and fluids. We use our teeth to **bite** off a piece of solid food. Then we **chew** it into smaller pieces so that we can swallow it. Different types of teeth do different parts of the job.

Jaw muscles produce the forces that cut and crush food. Forces acting on a small area will cut food more easily than forces acting on a large area. This is because the pressure is greater. So teeth for cutting are a bit like chisels.

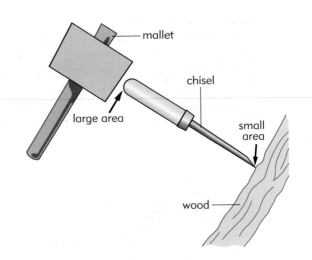

1 Look at the diagram.
   Why does the wood get cut, but not the mallet?

■ What are your teeth like?

The parts of your teeth that you normally see are called the crowns. They are covered in enamel, the hardest substance in your body. The roots are longer than the crowns. You can't see the roots because they are in your jawbone.

2 Look at the diagrams. Which of the two teeth is the better for biting off pieces of food?
   Explain your answer.

3 Which of the two types of teeth is better for the side-to-side movement of chewing?
   Explain your answer.

4 Why do you think your teeth are set so deeply in your jawbone?

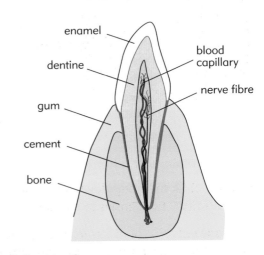

A front tooth.

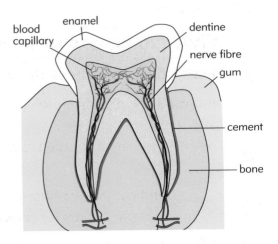

A back tooth.

So, all human teeth have the same basic structure, but their shapes are different. Their **shapes** suit the jobs that they do.

5 Look at the diagrams.
Then copy and complete the table.

Type of tooth	Function
incisors and _____	_____
premolars and _____	chewing and _____

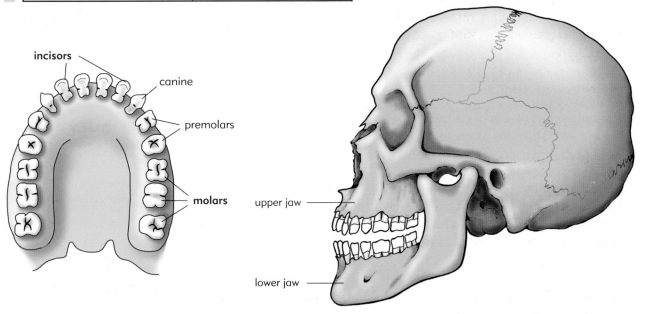

Cutting, then breaking down food and mixing it with saliva, makes food easier to swallow.

Humans eat a lot of different foods so our teeth are adapted for biting and chewing. But our teeth are unspecialised compared with the teeth of some other mammals.

What you need to remember [Copy and complete using the **key words**]

What's different about the way we feed?

Mammals use their teeth to _____ off pieces of food. Then they _____ it into smaller pieces before swallowing.

The _____ of the teeth are suited to their functions.

Humans use their:
- _____ and canines for biting
- _____ and pre-molars for chewing and crushing food.

[You need to be able to relate the shapes of teeth to their functions.]

9 Are all mammals' teeth the same?

Dogs can kill and eat other animals, so they are carnivores. Notice how pointed a dog's teeth are. They are specialised. They are adapted for a **carnivorous** diet.

Dogs need to hold on to prey without dislocating their jaws. So the joints between the skull and the lower jaw prevent side-to-side movement. Also, an up-and-down movement is best for cutting. The lower jaws move up and down in a **scissor-like** action. The front teeth can be held together to provide a strong grip.

The largest back teeth are adapted to cut or shear meat. They are called the carnassials. The upper and lower carnassial teeth work a bit like shears or scissors. The teeth behind them are flatter with cusps that bite together. They are a bit like a garlic crusher.

1 Look at the diagram.

   (a) In which direction does a dog's jaw move?

   (b) What prevents movements in other directions?

molars (flatter molars are for crushing)

carnassial teeth for cutting flesh

incisors for gripping

pre-molars

canines for gripping and tearing

Skull and lower jaw of a dog. Pointed teeth exert a lot of pressure.

Incisors meet to give a good grip.

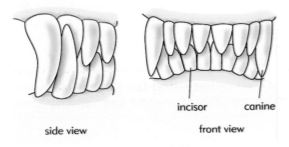

incisor   canine

side view   front view

These teeth give the dog a firm grip on its prey and help it to tear it.

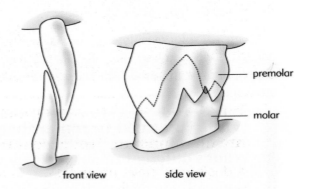

premolar

molar

front view   side view

Carnassial teeth cut or shear flesh like scissors.

2 (a) Explain how canine teeth are adapted to help a dog hold onto prey or meat and tear it apart.

   (b) Explain how the carnassial teeth are adapted to cut or shear meat as a dog chews.

3 Which teeth do you think are best adapted for crushing bones?

Can you tell what a mammal eats?

A mammal's teeth give you clues to its diet.

Plant-eating animals are called herbivores.
Their front teeth are adapted to cut plants, and
their back teeth to grind them up.

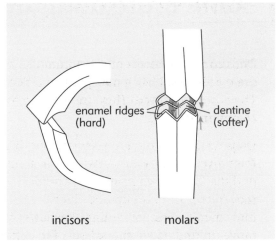

Herbivore incisors are sharp for cutting grass.
The molars and premolars have enamel ridges
for grinding.

4 Look at the pictures.
   What do you think:

   (a) animal **A** eats?

   (b) animal **B** eats?

   Explain your answers.

A

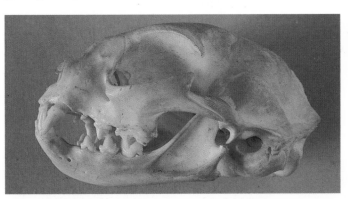

B

What you need to remember [Copy and complete using the **key words**]

Are all mammals' teeth the same?

A dog's jaws move up and down in a firm, _____-_____ action.
Its _____ are small but provide the good grip needed to pull meat apart.
Its sharp pointed _____ are useful for gripping and tearing.
Its _____ and _____ include the special, large _____ teeth.
It uses these teeth to cut meat and to crush bones.
All these features are adaptations for a _____ diet.

[You need to be able to relate (a) the shapes of teeth to the jobs that they do, and
(b) skulls and teeth to diet.]

H9 For Higher Tier students only

Some more adaptations to diet

The digestive systems of all mammals have the same basic parts.
But, like teeth, they are adapted to the animal's diet.

1 Your gut is a tube from your mouth to your anus.
Write down, in order, the main parts of this tube.

Some animals have shorter guts for their size than humans do.
Others have much longer guts for their size.

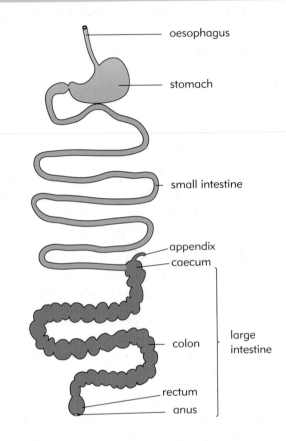

Human gut.

Cats have quite short guts. They eat meat and other foods that are rich in nutrients. Rabbits are about the same size as cats. But their guts are longer. Their food is far less nutritious than the cat's. So rabbits have to spend much more time eating and have to have room in their guts for much more food.

2 Write down <u>two</u> differences between gut **A** and gut **B**.

3 One of these is the gut of a cat, the other is from a rabbit.
Which is the cat?
Explain your answer.

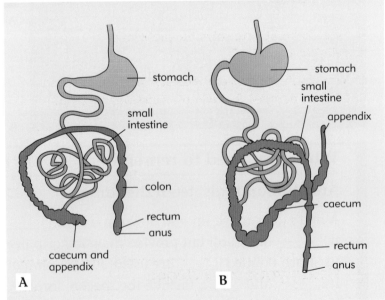

The problem of cellulose digestion

Mammals cannot make enzymes that digest **cellulose**. They make enzymes to digest only proteins, fats, and carbohydrates such as starch and maltose.

4 Why is the digestion of cellulose a problem for mammals?

5 Look at the diagram.
What is produced when cellulose is digested?

It doesn't matter to humans that we can't digest cellulose. We get plenty of nutrients from other foods. For us, the cellulose is useful dietary fibre. It gives the gut muscles something to push on.

For herbivores, however, it is a problem. Plant cell walls are made of cellulose. So cellulose makes up a large part of their diet. They need a way of digesting it.

Herbivores solve this problem by having **cellulose-digesting bacteria** and other microorganisms in their guts. The bacteria have enzymes that can break down the cellulose into sugars and other substances.

Parts of the guts of herbivores are adapted for these bacteria to live in. The part is different in different herbivores. You can find out more about these on pages 40–1.

6 How do herbivores solve the problem of cellulose digestion?

7 Why don't the guts of carnivores have special sections adapted for cellulose-digesting bacteria?

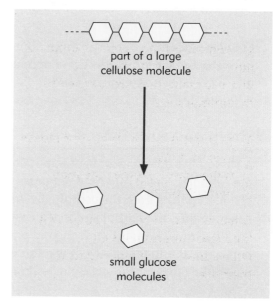

part of a large
cellulose molecule

small glucose
molecules

Cellulose is a very large molecule. Before it can be absorbed, it has to be broken down into smaller molecules.

Using your knowledge

1 Do you think the gut of a dog has a part adapted for cellulose digestion?
Explain your answer.

2 Termites are insects that feed on wood. This contains cellulose, but termites can't make enzymes to digest it.
Write down <u>two</u> features that termite guts must have.

H10 For Higher Tier students only
More about cellulose-digesting bacteria

Cellulose-digesting bacteria live in different parts of the gut in different herbivores. These parts are adapted to allow the bacteria to live and breed there.

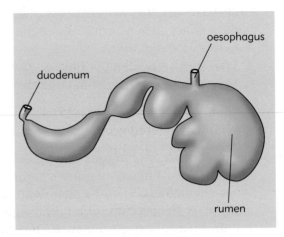

The rumen of sheep and cows provides a warm, moist home and plenty of food for the cellulose-digesting bacteria.

■ Sheep and cows have a rumen

A rumen is a special part between the oesophagus and the stomach. Sheep and cows eat grass and other plants. The food passes from the oesophagus into the rumen. After a while, the partially digested material is brought back up into the mouth and chewed again. Then it goes back into the rumen. It now has a larger surface area on which the bacteria can act, so digestion speeds up.

1 Draw a large copy of the rumen. Add arrows to show the first journey of the food in and out of the 'stomach'.
   In a different colour, add arrows to show the second journey of the food.

2 Where do cellulose-digesting bacteria live in sheep and cows?

3 Why do sheep and cows 'chew the cud'?

A lot of water and nutrients are absorbed in the first parts of the stomach. The final part is more like the stomach of other mammals. It secretes acid and proteases, so the bacteria that leave the rumen are killed and digested here. Many of them stay in the rumen to continue breaking down cellulose.

In a mutual relationship, both sides benefit. Sheep or cows and the cellulose-digesting bacteria both benefit from their relationship. So we call it **mutualism**.

4 Explain how a cow benefits from having bacteria in its rumen.

5 What benefits do the bacteria get from this relationship?

This cow is chewing the mixture from its rumen. We say it is 'chewing the cud'.

Rabbits have a large caecum and appendix

The home for cellulose-digesting bacteria in rabbits is made up of the **caecum** and **appendix**.

6 Look at the diagram.
Describe the position of the caecum and appendix in relation to the rest of the intestines.

Most absorption of food takes place in the small intestine. But digested food from the caecum also passes into the large intestine.
It then passes out of the body.

Rabbits actually pass two kinds of **faeces**. Those that came out of the caecum contain the digested cellulose that they need. They pass these in their burrows at night. Then they eat them. They pass the other kind of faeces outside their burrows during the day. They have absorbed the sugars and other nutrients from these, so they don't eat them.

7 Rabbits eat some of their faeces.

(a) Which kind do they eat?

(b) Why do they eat them?

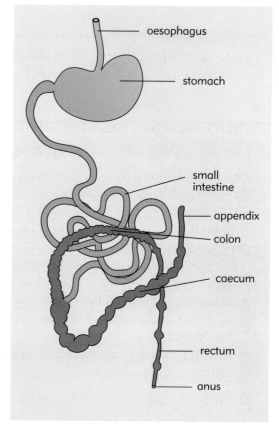

The digestive system of a rabbit.

Using your knowledge

1 Look at the diagram. Wombats are herbivores. Where do you think cellulose-digesting bacteria live in wombats? Explain your answer.

2 Rabbits and cellulose-digesting bacteria both benefit from their relationship. Write down a list of benefits for each of them.

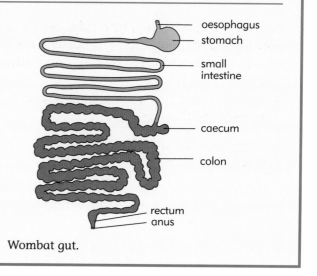

Wombat gut.

What causes decay and disease?

Ideas you need from *Humans as organisms*

■ Microorganisms such as bacteria and viruses can get into your body and cause disease.

■ It takes large numbers of microorganisms to make you ill.

■ The discovery of microorganisms

A Dutchman called Anton van Leeuwenhoek (1632–1723) was interested in using lenses for magnifying. It was hard for him to hold them steady, so he found a way of mounting the lens and the object so that they didn't wobble. He mounted the lens on a board and the object on a pointer. He used a screw arrangement to move the pointer so that the object was exactly the right distance from the lens to get a clear picture. This is what we call focusing.

1 Leeuwenhoek was the first person to see microorganisms. Why was this?

Leeuwenhoek invented this microscope. It was the first one that was good enough to see microorganisms.

■ Do microorganisms cause decay?

Leeuwenhoek saw microorganisms in sour milk, pond water and soil water. He called them 'little animals'. But he had no idea what they did. Some scientists thought that these 'little animals' made things decay. They did experiments to try to find out if getting rid of them stopped decay. They argued about whether they just appeared or came from somewhere.

2 The idea that microorganisms cause decay arose because of the sorts of places where Leeuwenhoek found them. Explain this.

A Frenchman called Louis Pasteur (1822–95) proved the connection between microorganisms and decay. His interest in microorganisms began when a winemaker asked him to find out why some of his wine was sour.

3 Look at the picture. Write down <u>two</u> things that Pasteur did to solve the problem of the sour wine.

Pasteur saw different microorganisms in the vats of good wine and bad wine. He did tests using these microorganisms and found that only the rod-shaped ones from the sour wine made wine go sour.

Pasteur showed that microorganisms made milk, wine, beer and other foods go bad. He also found a way of heat-treating them to kill the microorganisms without spoiling the taste. We call it pasteurisation. We still use it to stop our food going bad.

Where do the microorganisms come from?

Pasteur and other scientists argued about where microorganisms came from. A scientist called Lazzaro Spallanzani, who lived about 100 years before Pasteur, tried to show that microorganisms didn't just appear from nowhere.

He boiled flasks of broth to kill anything in them, and then sealed them. Nothing grew. But some scientists argued that nothing grew in them because the process of boiling and sealing had changed the air inside the flasks.

Pasteur thought that microorganisms must be everywhere and just settle on food from the air. He decided to do an experiment to test his idea. He realised that his flasks had to be open to the air.

Pasteur's experiment

Look at the diagrams. Pasteur's broth contained nutrients for the microorganisms to feed on.

4 What was the idea that Pasteur was testing?

5 Pasteur's flasks were open to the air. So why didn't the broth go bad?

6 Pasteur set up several flasks, not just one. Why?

Several months later the broth in his flasks was still fresh. Then Pasteur:

■ broke the necks of some flasks

■ tipped some flasks so that the broth went into the neck, then back into the flask.

7 If Pasteur's ideas are correct, what happens to the broth in each set of flasks? Explain your answers.

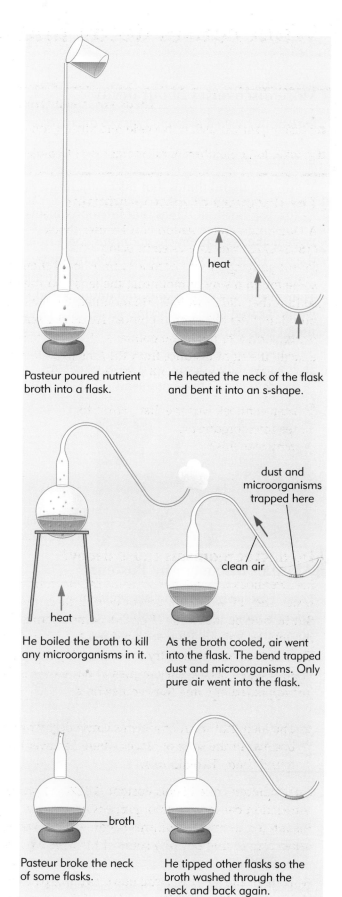

Pasteur poured nutrient broth into a flask.

He heated the neck of the flask and bent it into an s-shape.

heat

He boiled the broth to kill any microorganisms in it.

heat

dust and microorganisms trapped here

clean air

As the broth cooled, air went into the flask. The bend trapped dust and microorganisms. Only pure air went into the flask.

Pasteur broke the neck of some flasks.

broth

He tipped other flasks so the broth washed through the neck and back again.

What causes decay and disease? *continued*

More discoveries about decay

Pasteur discovered different types of microorganisms.

8 Write down:

(a) <u>two</u> useful things that microorganisms do

(b) <u>two</u> harmful things that microorganisms do.

Pasteur showed that microorganisms come from the air. They do not just appear from nowhere. Some are useful but others spoil or decay our food. They also decay dead plants and animals and their waste. As well as removing the waste, they recycle the useful substances in it.

9 If waste didn't decay, we'd have problems. Explain <u>two</u> of these problems.

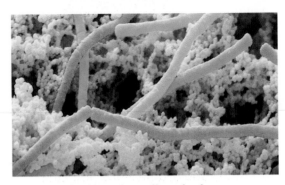

Lactobacilli make milk go bad.

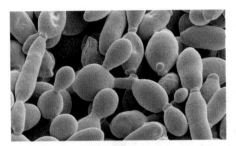

Yeast turns grape juice into wine.

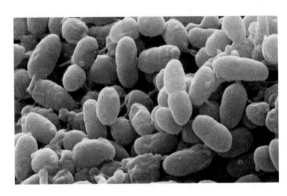

Acetobacter make vinegar.

Another discovery by Pasteur

Later, Pasteur was set another problem.
The silk industry was in trouble.
Something was killing the silkworms.

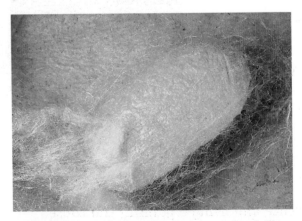

Silkworm caterpillars spin a cocoon made of silk.
This is where we get silk from.

This drawing of silkworms is from Pasteur's book *Diseases of silkworms*.

Pasteur spread the remains of diseased silkworms on these leaves. Healthy silkworms fed on the leaves and became diseased.

Pasteur killed a healthy silkworm and spread its remains on another set of leaves. Healthy silkworms fed on them and stayed healthy.

10 Look at the drawings of one of Pasteur's experiments. Copy and complete the flow chart.

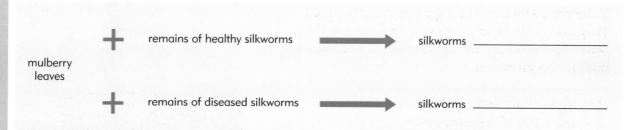

So, Pasteur had found that something in diseased silkworms caused disease in healthy animals. He found microorganisms in diseased silkworms, but not in healthy ones. He had made the connection between microorganisms and disease.

We call the microorganisms that cause disease **pathogens**. Pasteur worked on diseases of humans and other animals too. He published a scientific paper about his ideas of infections caused by microorganisms.

Other scientists read about his ideas. One of them was Joseph Lister. He was the surgeon who first used an antiseptic in his operating theatre. Antiseptics slow the growth of the microorganisms that cause infections. Before the use of antiseptics, one-third of patients died from infections following operations.

11 Explain how Joseph Lister's work supports Pasteur's theory that microorganisms can cause disease.

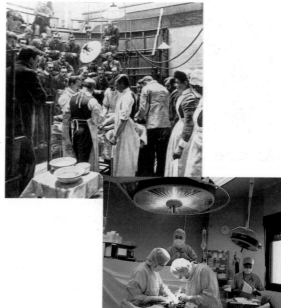

Operating theatres have changed in lots of ways.

What you need to remember [Copy and complete using the **key words**]

What causes decay and disease?

Microorganisms that cause disease are called _____.

[You need to be able to describe Pasteur's evidence that living organisms can cause decay and disease.]

How do we treat diseases?

When we are ill, we often take liquids or tablets called medicines. These contain useful **drugs**. Some of these drugs help to ease the symptoms of the disease. Others kill the **microorganisms** that cause the disease.

1 Look at the photographs then copy and complete the table.

	What it does	Examples
painkiller		
antibiotic		

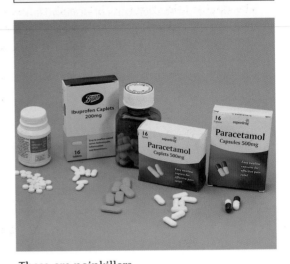

These are painkillers.
They relieve pain, but do not kill microorganisms.

Antibiotics don't work against all kinds of microorganisms. Penicillin, for example, kills some kinds of **bacteria** but not others. Other antibiotics kill different bacteria.

Antibiotics don't kill viruses. Viral pathogens live and reproduce inside cells. So it is hard to find drugs that kill **viruses** without damaging body cells and tissues.

These kill bacteria in the body.
We call them antibiotics.

Kelly and Roy both have influenza. The **symptoms** are a raised temperature, and aches and pains all over. Influenza is a virus infection. Roy also has a severe sore throat caused by a bacterial infection. This happened because Roy's body was weakened by the influenza virus and couldn't destroy the bacteria fast enough. So it is called a secondary infection.

The doctor told them both to rest, to keep warm and to drink plenty of fluids. She suggested taking **painkillers** such as paracetamol to ease the aches and pains. She warned them not to take too many.

2 The doctor also prescribed an antibiotic for Roy, but not for Kelly.
   Why is this?

3 (a) What is the maximum dose of paracetamol in one day?

   (b) Why is it dangerous to take more than this?

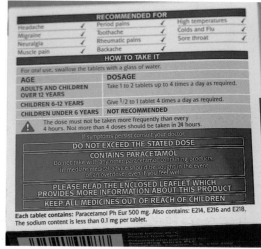

RECOMMENDED FOR		
Headache ✓	Period pains ✓	High temperatures ✓
Migraine ✓	Toothache ✓	Colds and Flu ✓
Neuralgia ✓	Rheumatic pains ✓	Sore throat ✓
Muscle pain ✓	Backache ✓	

HOW TO TAKE IT

For oral use, swallow the tablets with a glass of water.

AGE	DOSAGE
ADULTS AND CHILDREN OVER 12 YEARS	Take 1 to 2 tablets up to 4 times a day as required.
CHILDREN 6-12 YEARS	Give 1/2 to 1 tablet 4 times a day as required.
CHILDREN UNDER 6 YEARS	NOT RECOMMENDED

⚠ The dose must not be taken more frequently than every 4 hours. Not more than 4 doses should be taken in 24 hours.

If symptoms persist consult your doctor.

DO NOT EXCEED THE STATED DOSE

CONTAINS PARACETAMOL
Do not take with any other paracetamol-containing products. Immediate medical advice should be sought in the event of an overdose, even if you feel well.

PLEASE READ THE ENCLOSED LEAFLET WHICH PROVIDES MORE INFORMATION ABOUT THIS PRODUCT

KEEP ALL MEDICINES OUT OF REACH OF CHILDREN

Each tablet contains: Paracetamol Ph Eur 500 mg. Also contains: E214, E216 and E218. The sodium content is less than 0.1 mg per tablet.

An overdose of paracetamol is poisonous. It kills by damaging the liver and kidneys.

What you need to remember [Copy and complete using the **key words**]

How do we treat diseases?

Medicines contain useful _____.

Some of these drugs help to relieve _____ of the disease. For example _____ relieve aches and pains, but they do not kill the _____ that cause the disease.

To cure the disease, the _____ must be killed.

Antibiotics like penicillin kill _____ but not viruses inside the body.

Viruses live and reproduce inside cells.

So it is hard to find drugs that kill _____ without damaging body tissues.

Do antibiotics always work?

■ Why do we have lots of different antibiotics?

We need a **range** of different antibiotics because one antibiotic doesn't do every job.

■ Some antibiotics kill one type of bacterium and not others. The doctor usually knows which one to use to treat a particular infection.

■ Bacteria sometimes become **resistant** to one antibiotic. You need a different antibiotic to kill these bacteria.

■ Also some antibiotics make some people ill. If you are upset by, or are allergic to one antibiotic, the doctor needs to be able to give you a different one.

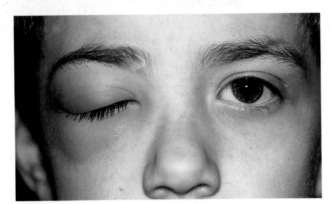

James has an eye infection. He is allergic to tetracycline.

1 Scientists continue to search for new antibiotics. Explain why we need:

(a) a range of different antibiotics

(b) new antibiotics.

2 One kind of penicillin that we used to cure throat infections no longer works.
Explain how this could have happened.

3 Look at the table.

(a) Write down <u>three</u> antibiotics that a doctor can prescribe to treat an eye infection.

(b) The doctor gave James a prescription for erythromycin.
Write down <u>one</u> reason for this choice.

4 Unfortunately the antibiotic did not cure James.
Write down <u>two</u> possible reasons.

Ideas you need from *Inheritance and selection*

Some strains of bacteria have become antibiotic-resistant.

■ In any population of bacteria there are different strains.

■ One strain may be resistant to a particular antibiotic.

■ The antibiotic kills the non-resistant strains.

■ The resistant strain survives and is able to reproduce.

■ The population of bacteria is now mainly resistant.

■ So the antibiotic is now no use against these bacteria.

This is an example of **natural selection**. It happens when we use antibiotics incorrectly or **over-use** them.
Then resistant bacteria have a better chance of surviving.

Unless you get worse, I won't give you an antibiotic.

Why?

Over-use of antibiotics leads to antibiotic resistance.

Antibiotic	Ear	Nose	Throat and mouth	Eye	Kidney and bladder
ampicillin	✓	✓	✓		✓
chloramphenicol	✓	✓	✓	✓	
erythromycin	✓	✓	✓	✓	
gentamycin				✓	✓
tetracycline	✓	✓	✓	✓	✓

The doctor then gave James a prescription for gentamycin. He told James that he must use all of it. That way there was less risk of the resistant **strain** of bacteria surviving.

5 Why must James finish his antibiotics? Explain as fully as you can.

A problem with tuberculosis

There are serious problems with some resistant bacteria. The bacteria that cause tuberculosis are hard to kill. An antibiotic called streptomycin was used successfully for many years. But the course of treatment lasted six months. So it was often used incorrectly. For example, many people stopped taking it too soon. So some of the bacteria survived, and these were the more resistant bacteria. These were passed on to other people.

6 Read the cutting from a Medical Research Council Update.

(a) What does multiple drug resistance mean?

(b) Why does the writer call it 'alarming'?

7 Now, TB is treated with a combination of four antibiotics for six months. Suggest why this is.

8 In New York, some people are paid to go to a clinic regularly to take their antibiotics. Suggest why the medical authorities decided to do this.

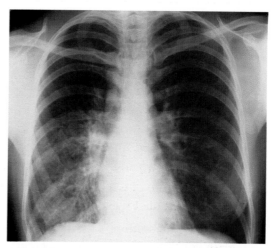

Tuberculosis (TB) is a lung infection.

Until recently, most strains of drug-resistant TB have been resistant to only one of the drugs available and so patients could be treated effectively using different drugs. But the emergence early this decade in New York City of multiple drug resistance is altogether more alarming. Patients were found to be infected with TB that was resistant to virtually all known drugs.

What you need to remember [Copy and complete using the **key words**]

Do antibiotics always work?

Bacteria can develop strains that are _____ to antibiotics as a result of _____ _____.

When one antibiotic no longer works against a particular _____ of bacterium, doctors have to prescribe a different antibiotic.

So to find the best antibiotic for treating a particular infection, we need to have a _____ of different antibiotics.

To slow down the rate at which bacteria become resistant, we should not _____ antibiotics.

Immunity and vaccination

■ How was vaccination discovered?

Edward Jenner (1749–1823) was a Gloucestershire doctor. He is usually credited with the discovery of vaccination against smallpox.

In fact, the Chinese used vaccination against smallpox 800 years before Jenner. It was also used in Turkey, Greece, England and India 100 years before Jenner. In England, Lady Mary Wortley Montague described what happened in Turkey and recommended vaccination to her friends in 1717.

The Jenner story goes something like this. There was an old wives' tale that dairymaids who caught cowpox from cows never got smallpox. Jenner thought that infecting people deliberately with cowpox might stop them getting smallpox.

In 1796, he took some pus from a cowpox spot and scratched it into the arm of a boy called James Phipps. Two months later, he tried to infect the boy with smallpox. He did not succeed because the boy was immune.

People feared smallpox. So following Jenner's experiment, vaccination against smallpox became common.

1 Jenner's experiment would not be allowed now. Why not?

2 Explain what happened in James Phipps' blood to make him immune to smallpox.

3 What clue does the story give you that the microorganisms which cause cowpox and smallpox are similar?

4 Suggest some reasons why Jenner usually gets the credit for discovering vaccination.

5 Look at the picture.
What does this tell you about what some people thought of vaccination?

> **Ideas you need from** *Humans as organisms*
>
> You can become **immune** to a disease as a result of:
>
> ■ having the disease
>
> ■ being **vaccinated** against it.
>
> In both cases, your **white blood cells** recognise the pathogen. They quickly make antibodies against it.
> The antibodies destroy the pathogens before they can make you ill.

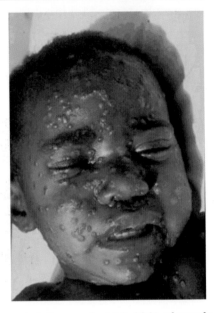

The spots left scars, but 12–30% of people who caught smallpox died.

More modern vaccines

Now we usually make vaccines from dead or inactive pathogens so they do not make us ill.

Proteins called **antigens** on the dead or inactive pathogens stimulate your white blood cells to make **antibodies** against them, just as they do against active pathogens. The antibodies react with or destroy the antigens. Later, if active pathogens of the same kind get into your blood, your white blood cells recognise them more quickly and make antibodies to destroy them.

We call this **active** immunity because your own cells are active against the pathogens.

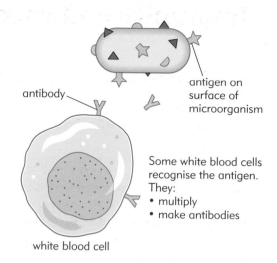

antibody

antigen on surface of microorganism

Some white blood cells recognise the antigen. They:
• multiply
• make antibodies

white blood cell

This is called the immune response.

6 Explain what happens when a vaccine gets into your blood.

7 Look at the pictures. Write down an example of a vaccine made from:

(a) dead bacteria

(b) weakened viruses.

8 Write down <u>two</u> ways of vaccinating people.

The **vaccine** in the drops is a weakened form of the polio virus.

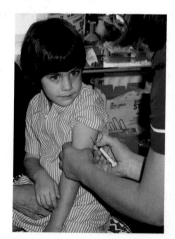

The vaccine being injected is made from dead whooping cough bacteria.

What you need to remember [Copy and complete using the **key words**]

Immunity and vaccination

You can be _____ against some diseases. Doctors and nurses use small amounts of dead or inactive forms of a pathogen as a _____.

In a vaccine, there are proteins from the pathogen called _____.

These stimulate white blood cells to produce _____ against these particular proteins.

The antibodies can react with and destroy the antigens.

If the same pathogen gets into your body in future, your _____ _____ _____ can respond by making the correct antibody straight away.

So vaccination has the same effect as having the disease, without making you ill.

It makes you _____ to the pathogen.

This is called _____ immunity because your own cells make the antibodies.

5 Vaccinations in childhood

Many childhood illnesses are caused by viruses. We cannot use antibiotics to treat virus infections, so we try to prevent them by vaccination.

■ Which diseases do we vaccinate against?

Viral pathogens like measles and rubella (German measles) are air-borne so they can spread very quickly. In the UK and many other countries, there is a vaccination programme for young children against many of these diseases.

1 What kind of immunity results from vaccination?

2 Write down <u>two</u> reasons why parents are encouraged to have their children vaccinated.

3 Why do some parents find it difficult to decide whether or not to have their children vaccinated?

■ The MMR vaccine

Look at the extract from a Health Education Authority leaflet about MMR.

4 Why is the vaccine called MMR?

Using the combined **vaccine** has both benefits and problems. Some health workers think that more children will be vaccinated if people have to make fewer visits to the clinic. Also, the combined vaccine is cheaper.

But other people think that the combined vaccine produces more side-effects than the separate vaccines. Also, some parents don't want their children vaccinated against measles because the measles vaccine causes fits in a few children. However, infection with measles is ten times more likely to cause fits than the vaccine.

5 Separate vaccines against measles, mumps and rubella are not available in the UK.

(a) Suggest why the health authorities decided to use only the combined MMR vaccine.

(b) Suggest why some parents are asking for the use of separate vaccines.

Vaccination doesn't just protect your child. If all children are vaccinated a disease has no-one to spread to.

But don't some children have side effects from the vaccine?

But some children are badly affected by diseases too. Some even die from them.

MMR vaccine

This is given when your child is between 12 and 15 months and again when your child is 3 to 5 years old.

The MMR vaccine protects your child against Measles, Mumps and Rubella (German Measles).

What is measles?
The measles virus is very infectious. It causes a high fever risk and a rash. About one in 15 children who get measles are at risk of complications which may induce chest infection, lung and brain damage. In severe cases measles can kill.

What is mumps?
The mumps virus causes swollen glands in the face. Before immunisation was introduced, mumps was the commonest cause of viral meningitis in children under 15. It can also cause deafness and swelling of the testicles in boys and ovaries in girls.

What is rubella?
Rubella, or German measles, is usually very mild and isn't likely to cause your children any problems. However if pregnant women catches it in her early pregnancy, it can harm the unborn baby.

Rubella is usually a mild disease.

6 (a) Why are girls offered vaccination against rubella when they are about 14 years old?

(b) Do all 14-year-old girls need to be vaccinated against rubella? Explain your answer.

Another kind of immunity

Sometimes you can't wait for your own white blood cells to make **antibodies**. One example is when a pregnant woman comes into contact with rubella. By the time she makes her own antibodies, the virus may have damaged her unborn child. So she is injected with antibodies to kill the virus. Her own cells are not active in making the antibodies, so we call this **passive** immunity.

7 Explain the difference between active and passive immunity.

There are other times when immediate protection is important. The rabies virus is a **dangerous pathogen** spread in the bite of an infected animal. The virus is so dangerous that it kills people before they have time to make their own antibodies. So, anyone bitten by a dog that may have rabies needs an injection of rabies antibodies straight away.

8 Does the injection of rabies antibodies produce active or passive immunity? Explain your answer.

9 We can be protected against some diseases by having injections of antibodies. Write down two sources of these antibodies.

* Human blood: Preparations made from the blood of thousands of people will definitely contain antibodies to common diseases such as Rubella.

* Animal blood: We use preparations of antibodies and antitoxins made from the blood plasma of vaccinated animals for treating less common conditions such as rabies and snake bite.

* Tissue culture: White blood cells don't grow for long in the test tube. But scientists can make them grow by joining them with special cells. Scientists separate out cells that make useful antibodies and grow pure cultures of those cells. Then they extract the antibodies from the culture.

Where antibodies and antitoxins come from.

What you need to remember [Copy and complete using the **key words**]

Vaccinations in childhood

There are vaccines to protect you against some _____ _____. Children are given the MMR _____ to protect them against measles, mumps and rubella (German measles). This is _____ _____.

If someone is exposed to a _____ _____ they need immediate protection. They are injected with the antibodies that destroy that pathogen. For example, someone bitten by a dog that may have rabies is injected with rabies _____. This is _____ immunity.

[You need to be able to discuss the advantages and disadvantages of being vaccinated against a particular disease.]

6

How has the treatment of disease changed?

Egyptians 4000 years ago knew about the problems of infection. They didn't know the causes, but they had some ways of treating them. They used myrrh, honey or an ore of copper called malachite to treat infected wounds. We now know that these substances slow down the growth of bacteria.

People in other countries and at other times also knew about infection and had some of their own remedies. Doctors used whatever treatments were fashionable at the time. Some worked, others didn't.

1 Look at the pictures. Write down <u>two</u> ways of treating infections that doctors no longer use.

Now, we know that microorganisms cause infectious diseases. With vaccination and the use of antibiotics, we expect to be better protected against them.
But millions of people die every year from infectious diseases. A worldwide vaccination programme got rid of smallpox. But other diseases continue to spread.

The fall and rise of tuberculosis (TB)

People in the UK used to call this disease 'consumption' because it seemed to consume the body. People with this disease lost weight, became weaker and seemed to waste away. As towns grew and overcrowding increased it became more and more common. At its worst, it caused as many a quarter of all deaths in Europe.

2 Look at the graph. As earnings rose, the number of deaths from tuberculosis fell. Suggest reasons for the link between earnings and infection.

3 Write down <u>one</u> reason why antibiotics were not the cause of this reduced death rate from tuberculosis.

Fresh air and a good diet were suggested as treatments for tuberculosis. Some patients were kept apart from other people, but tuberculosis was not beaten. Doctors hoped that penicillin would cure it, but that didn't work. Eventually an antibiotic called streptomycin was discovered. People had a good chance of being cured if they took it for six months. As a result of the discovery of streptomycin, the number of deaths from tuberculosis went down further.

Doctors do use leeches in medicine today, but not for treating infections.

Using nosegays.

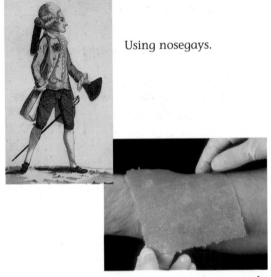

Honey was an ancient remedy. This modern dressing for infected wounds also contains honey.

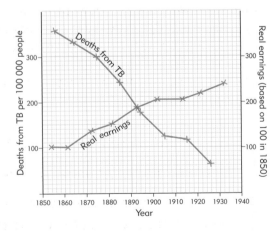

Deaths from TB before antibiotics and immunisation.

4 Suggest why fresh air and a good diet helped some patients.

5 What was the benefit of keeping tuberculosis patients away from other people?

6 Look at the pictures. Write down <u>four</u> reasons why deaths from tuberculosis are increasing.

7 AIDS is a major cause of the spread of tuberculosis.
Explain this as fully as you can.

8 In 1993, the World Health Organisation declared that tuberculosis was a global emergency.
What do you think they meant?

Prevention is better than cure

We can prevent many infectious diseases by vaccination. Some vaccines work better than others. The TB vaccine doesn't always work. In some people the immunity caused by vaccination against tuberculosis lasts for only a few years. Many people have never been vaccinated against it. So there are plenty of people for the disease to spread to.

9 Write down <u>two</u> reasons why vaccination against tuberculosis has not stopped its spread.

Although we have used vaccination for much longer, it is only in the past 50 years that scientists have found out how the immune response works. They are using this knowledge to try to develop new and better vaccines.

10 Why do we need to find a better vaccine against tuberculosis?

Reasons for the increase in TB include:

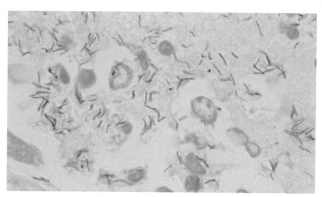

a Some strains of TB are now antibiotic resistant.

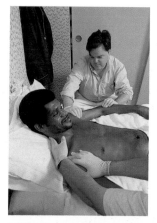

b The immune systems of AIDS patients do not work properly.

c TB spreads where there is overcrowding, poverty and homelessness.

d Recycling air in aircraft can spread infections like TB.

What you need to remember

How has the treatment of disease changed?

[You do not need to remember the story on pages 54 and 55. But when you are given information, you need to be able to explain how treatment of disease has changed as a result of increased understanding of antibiotics and immunity.]

H1 For Higher Tier students only

More about the immune response

■ What are antigens?

The proteins on the surfaces of different living things vary. Because these proteins vary, your white blood cells can recognise the ones that don't belong in your body. We call them antigens.

Ideas you need from *Humans as organisms*

■ Your blood contains several kinds of white blood cells. They protect your body against pathogens and other 'foreign' materials.

■ Some white cells take in and digest the pathogens. Others make antibodies against them.

■ You become immune as a result of vaccination or having a disease.

1 Look at the diagram.

   (a) How many different proteins can you see on the bacterium?

   (b) Are all the proteins antigens? Explain your answer.

The proteins coloured red cause an immune response. So they are antigens.

■ How do we destroy antigens?

White blood cells called lymphocytes destroy antigens. The response to antigens is called the immune response.

One kind of lymphocyte is called a T-cell. It reacts with and destroys cells with antigens on their surface. Viruses leave their protein coats on the surface membranes of cells. So T-lymphocytes detect cells infected with viruses and kill them.

Another kind of lymphocyte is called a B-cell. It secretes antibodies to destroy the antigens in the blood. Each type of B-cell makes antibodies against only one kind of antigen. We say that antibodies are specific to one kind of antigen.

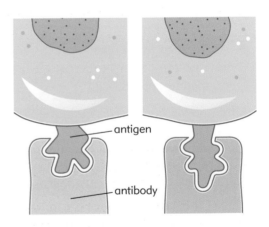

2 Write down <u>two</u> kinds of lymphocytes that are involved in the immune response.

3 Look at the antibodies in the picture.

   (a) Each antibody works against only one kind of antigen. Why is this?

   (b) Which antibody works against antigen X?

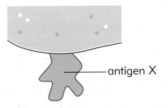

The shape of an antibody matches the shape of the antigen.

A newborn baby has millions of different types of B-cells. But there are only a few of each kind. When T-cells recognise an antigen, they stimulate the right kind of B-lymphocytes to divide. They produce identical cells, so they are clones.

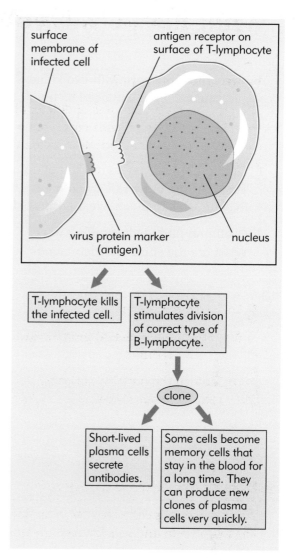

surface membrane of infected cell

antigen receptor on surface of T-lymphocyte

virus protein marker (antigen)

nucleus

T-lymphocyte kills the infected cell.

T-lymphocyte stimulates division of correct type of B-lymphocyte.

clone

Short-lived plasma cells secrete antibodies.

Some cells become memory cells that stay in the blood for a long time. They can produce new clones of plasma cells very quickly.

4 Look at the diagram.
Then copy and complete the sentences.

T-cells have _____ on their surface _____ that recognise and attach to antigens on a cell's surface. They can then destroy cells that have these _____.

When T-cells recognise an antigen, they also stimulate the right kinds of ___-lymphocytes to multiply and form _____.

The cells of a clone are _____. Each cell can secrete about 2000 antibodies per second. The antibodies destroy _____ in the blood.

5 You develop immunity the first time a particular antigen gets into your blood. Write down <u>two</u> things that can happen to you to set off this immune response.

The number of B-cells falls when an infection is over. But some B-cells, called memory cells, stay in the body.

6 Explain why antibodies are produced very rapidly when an antigen enters the body for a second time.

Using your knowledge

1 It is hard for your body to destroy viruses because they live inside your cells. The whole cell has to be destroyed. Explain how lymphocytes help you to overcome a virus infection.

2 Antibodies are specific to one type of antigen. But vaccination with the cowpox virus makes us immune to smallpox. What does this tell us about the cowpox and the smallpox viruses?

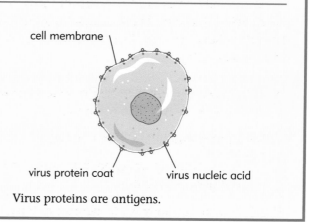

cell membrane

virus protein coat

virus nucleic acid

Virus proteins are antigens.

What happens if your kidneys fail?

You were probably born with two kidneys. In some people, one kidney is damaged by injury or disease and it no longer works. This is not a problem if the other kidney remains healthy.

1 Tina lost one kidney as a result of an accident. There was no other serious damage. Explain why Tina can live a normal life.

2 Geoff and Rita's kidneys don't work. What are the effects on their blood?

Ideas you need from *Maintenance of life*

■ You digest proteins and absorb the amino acids produced.

■ Your liver makes urea when it breaks down excess amino acids.

■ **Urea** is poisonous so your kidneys excrete it from your body.

■ Your kidneys also control the balance of water and salts in your body.

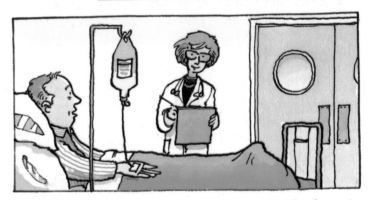

Geoff's kidneys failed when he had a heart attack. The doctor is treating him with drugs to start his kidneys working again. She thinks that he will get better.

■ What can be done for Rita?

Rita is having **dialysis**. The dialysis machine is taking out poisonous urea and the excess water and salts from her blood. It takes about 10 hours. She has this treatment three times a week. She has to have a low protein, low salt diet. Also, she musn't take in too much fluid.

3 Dialysis machines are sometimes called kidney machines. Why is this?

4 Rita has to eat a low protein diet. Explain this as fully as you can.

5 Write down <u>two</u> other problems of kidney dialysis as a treatment.

6 The amount of urea in most people's blood probably doesn't vary very much. The amount in Rita's blood varies a lot. Why is this?

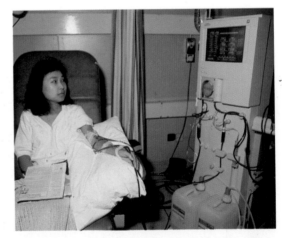

Rita had a kidney infection. Both kidneys were damaged. They will not recover.

What happens when Rita has dialysis?

When Rita has dialysis, her blood goes through the machine then back into her body. The machine, all the needles and the tubes have to be sterile. They must have no microorganisms in them to cause infection.

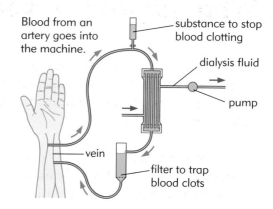

Blood from an artery goes into the machine.

substance to stop blood clotting

dialysis fluid

pump

vein

filter to trap blood clots

Rita's blood must not clot in the machine. A clot in her blood could kill her.

7 Look at the diagram, then copy and complete the sentences:

Rita's blood goes out of an _____ into the machine.

It goes back into her body in a _____.

8 New sterile needles, tubes and filters are used for every dialysis treatment. Why is this?

9 Blood clots when it comes out of your body. Explain how the problem of clotting is solved in dialysis.

What happens inside the machine?

The **partially permeable membranes** inside the machine let small molecules like glucose, urea and salts through. They don't let cells or large molecules such as proteins through. Substances that can pass through the membranes diffuse from a high concentration to a low concentration. After dialysis the **concentration** of dissolved substances in the blood is normal.

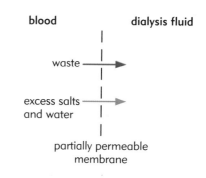

blood   dialysis fluid

waste

excess salts and water

partially permeable membrane

10 Write down two substances that pass into the dialysis fluid.

11 Write down two ways of making sure that the blood goes back into Rita's body at 37 °C.

There is an enormous surface area of dialysis tubing in the machine. The dialyser is enclosed in insulating material.

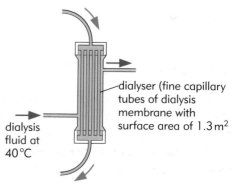

dialyser (fine capillary tubes of dialysis membrane with surface area of 1.3 m²)

dialysis fluid at 40 °C

What you need to remember [Copy and complete using the **key words**]

What happens if your kidneys fail?

If your kidneys fail, you cannot get rid of poisonous _____ from your blood.

Some people are treated by regular _____ on a machine.

In a dialysis machine, urea passes from the blood into dialysis fluid across _____ _____ _____.

Regular treatment is needed. After dialysis, the amount of urea starts to rise.

The next treatment restores the _____ of dissolved substances to normal levels.

8 Problems of kidney transplants

Remember, Rita has to have regular dialysis. Unless she can have a kidney **transplant**, she will need dialysis for the rest of her life. In a kidney transplant, a **diseased kidney** is replaced with a healthy one from a donor.

1 What differences would a successful kidney transplant make to Rita's life?

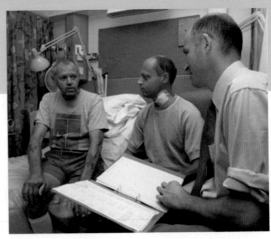

Steve has recovered from the operation to remove one of his kidneys. The kidney is now working in his brother's body.

Where do replacement kidneys come from?

The healthy kidneys usually come from people who have just died. Kidneys can only be used if the person wished it and their relatives agree to donate them. So there are more people waiting for transplants than there are kidneys available. In the year 2000 in the UK, 4891 people were waiting for a kidney transplant but only 1360 received a new kidney.

2 Explain how 680 people willing to donate kidneys after their deaths can provide 1360 people with a new kidney.

3 A few kidneys come from live donors. Live donors are usually close relatives. What are the risks for a live donor?

Do transplanted kidneys always work?

Kidneys usually start to work soon after they are transplanted. The problems come later.

4 Look at the graph. During which 3-month period following a transplant is the kidney most likely to fail?

5 What percentage of kidneys transplanted from a non-related donor are still working after 2 years?

Kidneys fail because they are **rejected**. Rejection happens when the body's **immune** system recognises that some proteins in the new kidney are foreign. They are antigens, so white blood cells destroy them.

6 What do we mean when we say that a kidney is rejected?

7 Describe the difference between rejection rates for kidneys from related and non-related donors.

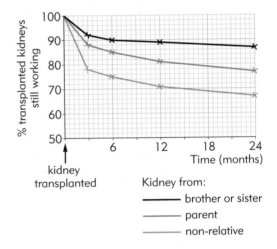

Graph showing % transplanted kidneys still working vs Time (months), with lines for kidney from: brother or sister, parent, non-relative.

Kidney from:
— brother or sister
— parent
— non-relative

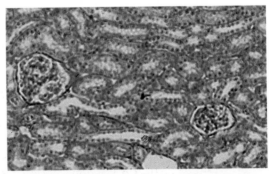

Healthy kidney tissue.

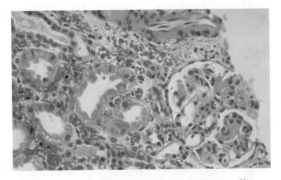

Antibodies are destroying these kidney cells.

Can we prevent rejection?

When a kidney donor and the recipient are related, more of the body proteins are likely to be similar than when they are not related. We say that related people have a similar 'tissue type'. So a kidney from a relative is less likely to be rejected than one from an unrelated donor.

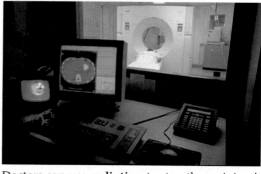

Doctors can use **radiation** to stop the recipient's bone marrow making white blood cells.

8 Explain why hospitals try to match the 'tissue type' of donor and recipient as closely as possible.

Only transplants between identical twins produce a perfect match of tissue type. So doctors try to stop the immune system of the recipient working so well.

These drugs stop white blood cells multiplying. So they **suppress** the immune response.

9 Why do doctors suppress the immune response of transplant patients?

10 Look at the photographs. Write down <u>two</u> ways of suppressing the immune response.

11 Transplant patients must not come into contact with any infections for a while after their transplant. Explain this as fully as you can.

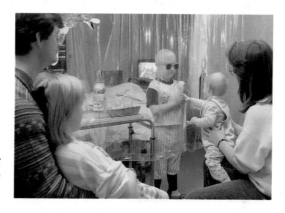

Patients easily catch infections when their immune systems are suppressed. So they are kept in **sterile** conditions after a transplant.

What you need to remember [Copy and complete using the key words]

Problems of kidney transplants

If a suitable donor can be found, a _____ _____ can be replaced with a healthy one. This is called a kidney _____. But transplanted kidneys can be _____ by the _____ system of the recipient.

Some precautions to prevent rejection are to:

- match the '_____ _____' of the donor and recipient as closely as possible
- treat the bone marrow of the recipient with _____ to stop white blood cell production
- keep the recipient in _____ conditions for some time after the transplant
- treat the recipient with drugs that _____ the immune response.

[You need to be able to evaluate the advantages and disadvantages of treating kidney failure by dialysis or kidney transplant.]

H2 For Higher Tier students only
More about dialysis

A Dutchman called Willem Kolff invented the first kidney machine in 1943. The patient's blood went through a cellophane filter in a water bath. He used it to keep people alive for a short time in the hope that their own kidneys would recover. Long-term use caused too much damage to blood vessels.

In 1960, an American called Bolding Scribner found a safer way of connecting patients to kidney machines. Long-term dialysis then became possible.

1 Look at the diagram.
   Write down <u>two</u> things that cannot pass through the filter.

2 If we use water as the dialysis fluid, glucose and mineral ions pass out of the patient's blood. Also, water passes into the blood. Why don't we want these things to happen?

Instead of using water, we use dialysis fluid containing glucose and mineral ions in the same concentration as in normal blood. So glucose diffuses into the blood at the same rate that it diffuses out – there is no net loss of glucose from the blood.

A kidney patient's blood contains excess water and mineral ions. So these diffuse out of the blood faster than they diffuse in. We say that there is a net loss of water and mineral ions from the blood. Once the water–mineral ion balance in the blood is correct, there is no further net loss of water and ions.

3 Why is the concentration of glucose and mineral ions in dialysis fluid the same as that in normal blood?

4 Write down <u>two</u> dissolved substances that are lost from the blood into the dialysis fluid.

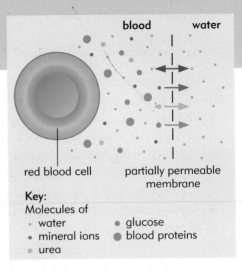

red blood cell   partially permeable membrane

Key:
Molecules of
· water   • glucose
• mineral ions   ● blood proteins
○ urea

In dialysis, small molecules pass through the filter but large molecules don't. The first kidney machine worked like this.

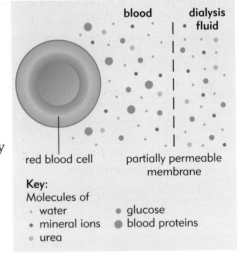

red blood cell   partially permeable membrane

Key:
Molecules of
· water   • glucose
• mineral ions   ● blood proteins
○ urea

Now dialysis fluid contains the same concentration of glucose and mineral ions as normal blood.

Using your knowledge

1 Copy and complete the graph.

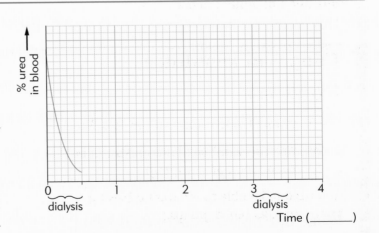

Graph to show the changes in the percentage of _____ in a dialysis patient's plasma over a four-day period.

H3 For Higher Tier students only
Blood transfusions

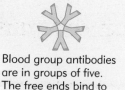
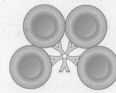

Blood group antibodies are in groups of five. The free ends bind to **antigens** on the surface of red blood cells...

...so they can clump red blood cells together.

During and after operations such as kidney transplants, people sometimes lose a lot of blood. They may need to be given extra blood from a donor. We call this a **blood transfusion**. Doctors can't just use any human blood. It has to be the right **blood group**. When blood transfusions were first tried, many people died. Doctors didn't know that there were different types of blood.

1 People have a test to find out their blood group before an operation or having a baby. Why is this?

We now know that if the blood of the donor and recipient do not match, red blood cells clump together. This is called **agglutination**. Clumps of red cells block blood vessels and the person dies.

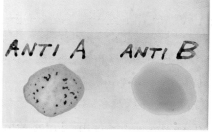

Anti-A agglutinates group A blood, but anti-B doesn't.

The ABO blood grouping system

There are several blood group systems. Matching with the ABO blood grouping system is the most important. An Austrian called Karl Landsteiner discovered it in 1901. Antibodies in the recipient's blood clump red cells of the wrong type. The donor's plasma doesn't affect the recipient's cells. It gets too diluted to do any damage.

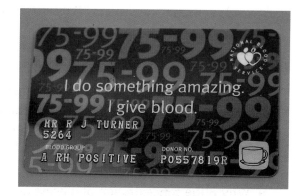

I do something amazing.
I give blood.
MR R J TURNER
5264
BLOOD GROUP   A RH POSITIVE
DONOR NO.   P0557819R

2 Look at Mr Turner's blood group card. What is his blood group?

3 Explain why Landsteiner's discovery is important.

4 Explain what will happen if Mr Turner has a transfusion of group B blood.

Blood group	antigen on red blood cells	antibody in plasma
A	A	anti-B
B	B	anti-A
AB	A and B	none
O	none	anti-A and anti-B

Using your knowledge

1 Explain why:

(a) group O blood can be given to anyone

(b) a person with blood group AB can be given blood of any group.

[You need to be able to interpret tables for matching ABO blood groups.]

Blood group	Can give blood to	Can have blood from
A	A and AB	A and O
B	B and AB	B and O
AB	AB	any group
O	any group	O

Some groups of microorganisms

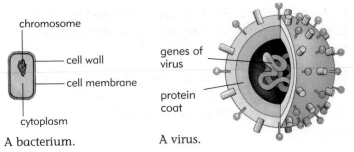

Ideas you need from *Humans as organisms*

- Bacteria have cell walls, cell membranes and cytoplasm, but their genes are not in a nucleus.

- Viruses are even smaller than bacteria. They have a few genes in a protein coat. They are harmful because they can reproduce only inside living cells.

Note: the bacterium and virus are drawn to different scales.

chromosome

cell wall

cell membrane

cytoplasm

A bacterium.

genes of virus

protein coat

A virus.

Some fungi are microorganisms

Scientists put moulds, yeasts and mushrooms in the same group because they have some things in common.

- They do not contain chlorophyll, so they cannot make their own food.

- They all feed by digesting and absorbing organic materials made by other organisms.

Moulds and yeasts are **fungi**.

1 Write down the group that moulds and yeasts belong to.

Although they belong to the same group, the structure of moulds and yeasts is different.

2 Write down <u>four</u> parts that both yeasts and moulds have.

3 Copy and complete the sentences:

Yeasts are made of separate cells.
Each cell has a _____.
Moulds are made of _____.
Each hypha has walls around its cytoplasm, but it is not separated into _____.
The cytoplasm contains many _____.

Moulds reproduce asexually by producing **spores**.

4 Copy the diagram of the yeast cell. Underline the names of the parts that are also in bacteria.

5 Write down <u>two</u> ways that both yeasts and bacteria are different from viruses.

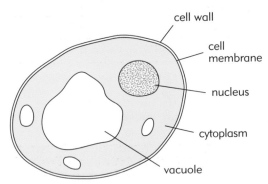

cell wall

cell membrane

nucleus

cytoplasm

vacuole

Yeasts are **single-celled** organisms.

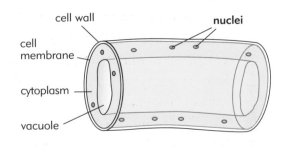

cell wall

nuclei

cell membrane

cytoplasm

vacuole

small part of a hypha

Moulds are made of threads called **hyphae**. One thread is a called a hypha.

■ Making use of microorganisms

Humans have used microorganisms for thousands of years for making food and drink.

In the Middle East, they used them 5000 years ago to make alcohol. Different cultures developed different alcoholic drinks depending on the plants from which they got their sugars.

Yoghurt was made in India nearly 2000 years ago. Turning milk into yoghurt and cheese was a way of turning milk into something that would keep for a longer time.

Now we use lots of foods made with the help of microorganisms. We sometimes call them fermented foods. The picture of the ploughman's lunch shows some that you may have tried.

Ideas you need from
Humans as organisms

Microorganisms:

■ grow slowly in cold conditions

■ grow faster in warm conditions

■ die if the temperature rises too high.

6 Copy and complete the table.

Food or drink	Type of microorganism
bread	yeast
white cheese	
	bacteria and mould
yoghurt	
beer	
vinegar	

Yeast cells help us to make beer and bread. We use bacteria to make **cheese**, yoghurt and the vinegar for the pickle. **Moulds** make some cheeses 'blue'.

What you need to remember [Copy and complete using the **key words**]

Some groups of microorganisms

We use:

■ bacteria to make _____ and _____

■ _____ to give blue cheeses their colour and flavour

■ _____ to make bread and alcoholic drinks.

Moulds and yeasts are _____. They have cell walls, cell membranes, cytoplasm and nuclei. Yeast is a _____-_____ organism, so each cell has one nucleus.

Moulds are made of threads called _____ and each hypha has many nuclei.

Moulds produce _____ to reproduce asexually.

[You need to be able to compare the structure of moulds and yeasts with viruses and bacteria.]

Using yeast to make wine and beer

Like you, yeasts use carbohydrates as an energy source. They produce **ethanol** (alcohol) by **anaerobic** respiration of sugars. We call the process **fermentation**. So we use yeasts to ferment sugars to make alcoholic drinks such as beer and wine.

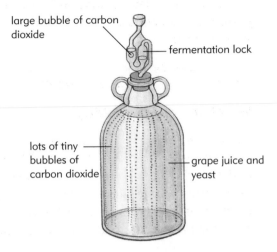

large bubble of carbon dioxide

fermentation lock

lots of tiny bubbles of carbon dioxide

grape juice and yeast

The sugars in the grape juice in the demijohn are fermenting.

■ Making wine

1 Look at the picture. Where do:

(a) the bubbles of carbon dioxide come from?

(b) the sugars for making wine come from?

2 Copy and complete the word equation:

sugars → ethanol (_____) + carbon _____ + some 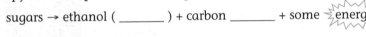 energy

3 Explain why we need to:

(a) let carbon dioxide out of the demijohn

(b) stop oxygen going in

(c) stop microorganisms going in.

4 Look at the picture.
Then copy and complete the table.

Source of sugar	Alcoholic drink
grape juice	_____
_____	cider
pears	_____

We make cider from apples, perry from pears and wine from fruits such as grapes.

■ Where do the sugars in beer come from?

We make beer using malt sugar.
This comes from the starch in **barley**.

5 What is barley?

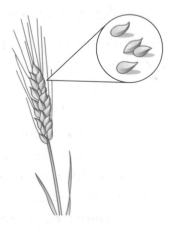

Barley grains are the seeds of barley plants.

Brewing beer

To start the breakdown of starch, we soak the barley grains in water. The grains swell up and begin to germinate. Enzymes start to change the stored starch into malt sugar.

$$\text{starch} \xrightarrow{\text{enzymes}} \text{malt sugar (maltose)}$$

We call this process **malting**.

The brewer dries and crushes the grains and soaks them in hot water to dissolve the **sugars**. Then he adds hops and boils the mixture. Next he removes the hops, cools the solution and lets it into the fermenting vessel. From the time the brewer adds the yeast, it takes about five days to ferment the sugars to alcohol.

He matures different beers in different ways.

6 Water, barley, yeast and hops are raw materials for making beer.
   What is the purpose of each of these ingredients?

7 What are hops?

8 Why does the brewer cool the solution <u>before</u> adding the yeast?

9 There is five times as much yeast at the end of the process as there was at the start. Why is this?

The extra yeast is not wasted. It is made into vitamin tablets or yeast extracts such as Marmite.

How hops grow.

Hop 'cones'.

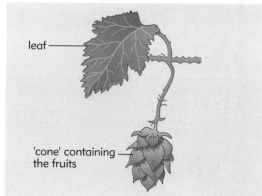

leaf

'cone' containing the fruits

We use hop 'cones' to give beer its **bitter** taste.

What you need to remember [Copy and complete using the **key words**]

Using yeast to make wine and beer

Yeast cells use carbohydrates as an energy source. They produce _____ when they have no oxygen.

$$\text{sugar} \xrightarrow{\text{yeast}} \text{ethanol (alcohol)} + \text{carbon dioxide} + \text{some energy}$$

This is the word equation for _____ respiration in yeast. We call it _____.
In wine making, the yeast uses the natural sugars in grapes.
In brewing, the carbohydrates come from _____ grains. Enzymes in the grains break down starch to sugars in a process called _____. The _____ are dissolved in water and fermented. Hops give the beer its _____ flavour.

67

Using yeast for baking

Yeast gets its energy by breaking down sugars in respiration. It respires faster in **warm** conditions.

It can **respire**:

- with oxygen (aerobically):

    sugar + oxygen → carbon dioxide + water + energy

- without oxygen (anaerobically):

    sugars → ethanol + carbon + some energy
         (alcohol) dioxide

This is how we make bread dough.

In both cases, **yeast** produces waste carbon dioxide.
We use this **carbon dioxide** when we make bread.
The **bubbles** of carbon dioxide are trapped in the dough.
The bubbles **expand** as the dough bakes.
So bread is light and spongy.

1 List the ingredients of bread dough.

2 Look at the table.

Place	Time for dough to rise
refrigerator	24 hours
cold room	overnight
room temperature	2 hours
warm place	1 hour

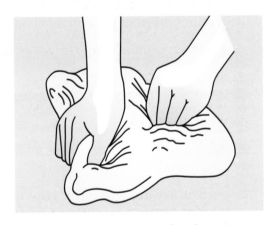

After we knead it, we leave dough to rise.

(a) What is the effect of temperature on the time it takes for dough to rise?

(b) Explain the reason for this effect.

To make a loaf, we shape the dough and put it into a tin. Then we let it rise again before we bake it.

Put dough in the tin.

Leave in a warm place. (25 to 30 °C)

bubbles of carbon dioxide make the dough rise

Bake in a hot oven. (230 °C)

Different types of bread

Bread made with yeast.

Bread made with yeast

3 Look at the bread. Describe <u>two</u> processes that helped to make it light.

4 Why are there no living yeast cells in a loaf of bread?

Soda bread

We use sodium bicarbonate (baking soda) to make soda bread. Baking soda produces the bubbles of carbon dioxide that make it rise.

Soda bread.

Unleavened bread

Sometimes bread is made without yeast or baking soda. We call it unleavened bread.

5 Which has the lighter texture, a slice of soda bread or unleavened bread? Explain your answer.

6 (a) What is the recipe for?

(b) Why is it best to leave the circles to stand before baking?

Unleavened bread.

Recipe

1 Mix together 200 g plain flour, 1 teaspoon of salt and 1 tablespoon of oil.
2 Blend 10 g of fresh yeast with $\frac{1}{4}$ pint of warm water.
3 Mix the liquid into the flour and knead it until it is smooth and stretchy.
4 Cover the dough with a clean, damp cloth and leave it to rise.
5 Flatten the dough, brush it with oil and roll it up. Then divide it into four.
6 Roll each piece into a flat circle. Top the pieces with tomato puree, herbs, tomato and cheese.
7 Let it stand for 30 minutes, then bake it at gas Mark 8 for 25 minutes.

What you need to remember [Copy and complete using the **key words**]

Using yeast for baking

To get enough energy to grow and reproduce, yeast needs to _____ aerobically. But it can also respire anaerobically. This releases less energy. Both kinds of respiration release _____ _____ gas.

In baking, we mix flour, sugar, _____ and water to make dough. Then we leave it somewhere _____ to rise. The yeast cells respire and produce _____ of carbon dioxide, so the bread rises. The bubbles _____ when the bread is baked. This makes the bread 'light'.

How we make yoghurt and cheese

Milk contains plenty of nutrients suitable for microorganisms. If we grow the right microorganisms in it, we can use them to change the milk into yoghurt or cheese.

We usually start to make cheese or yoghurt by pasteurising the milk. This kills any pathogens and other unwanted microorganisms, but it does not spoil the taste.

Milk is held at 72 °C for 25 seconds. We call this pasteurisation.

1 Why do we pasteurise milk?

2 How do we pasteurise milk?

3 You can buy some cheeses made from unpasteurised milk. Why do some people want to ban them?

There are some bacteria even in pasteurised milk. If you leave a bottle of pasteurised milk unopened in a warm place, these bacteria turn it sour.

4 There are normally some bacteria left in pasteurised milk. What do they do?

We need to use different bacteria to make each kind of cheese or yoghurt. Dairies produce and test cultures of these bacteria. They make sure that the bacteria are in the correct proportions. A culture like this is called a **starter culture**. A poor starter culture results in a poor product.

curds

whey

We can strain the curds from the whey to make a soft cheese.

5 What is special about a starter culture?

▊Yoghurt

The starter culture for making yoghurt contains equal amounts of two different bacteria.

6 Describe the shapes of the two bacteria in yoghurt starter culture.

Starter culture for yoghurt.

How do yoghurt bacteria work?

The bacteria feed on a sugar called lactose in the milk. They produce **lactic acid** as a waste product. Lactic acid lowers the pH of the milk to 4.6. It becomes so acid that the **milk proteins** clot. The clotted proteins or curds that yoghurt bacteria produce are soft. So yoghurt is solid, but fairly smooth and soft.

7 What is the pH of yoghurt?

8 Describe the effect of a low pH on milk proteins.

You can make yoghurt at home using natural yoghurt as a starter culture.

9 Look at the pictures. Then copy and complete the flow chart.

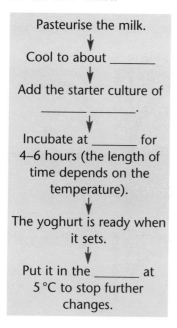

Pasteurise the milk.
↓
Cool to about _____
↓
Add the starter culture of
_____ _____ .
↓
Incubate at _____ for 4–6 hours (the length of time depends on the temperature).
↓
The yoghurt is ready when it sets.
↓
Put it in the _____ at 5 °C to stop further changes.

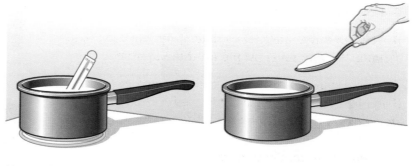

Heat a pint of milk to about 90 °C. Do not let it boil. Then cool it to about 40 °C.

Stir in a tablespoon of natural yoghurt. Don't kill the bacteria by adding them while the milk is too hot.

Cover it and leave somewhere warm overnight, or keep it warm in a vacuum flask.

When it has set, put it in the refrigerator.

10 Why do we:

(a) cool the milk to 40 °C?

(b) incubate at 40 °C?

11 Changes to the yoghurt stop when you put it into the refrigerator. Why is this?

What you need to remember [Copy and complete using the key words]

How we make yoghurt and cheese

To make yoghurt, we add a _____ _____ of bacteria to warm milk.
The bacteria ferment the milk sugar (lactose) to produce _____ _____ .
The lactic acid clots the _____ _____ , solidifying the milk into yoghurt.

More about making cheese

The start of cheese making is similar to the start of yoghurt making. But the starter culture is **different**.

The bacteria in the starter culture make curds that are more solid than yoghurt curds. So the milk separates into **curds** and **whey**. Most cheese makers add rennet to speed up the clotting. Rennet is an enzyme.

1 What are curds and whey?

2 Look at the flow chart. Write down <u>two</u> things that help to make curds and whey.

> **REMEMBER**
>
> We pasteurise milk before we make it into yoghurt. Then we cool it and add a starter culture.

We make cheese from curds. We use whey as animal food, to make syrups or to grow yeasts.

When the milk has separated, the whey is drained off.

Cutting the curds lets more whey drain out.

The cheese-maker mills the curds to break them up. Then he presses them into moulds.

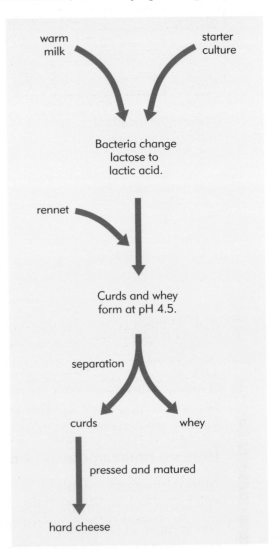

warm milk → starter culture →

Bacteria change lactose to lactic acid.

rennet →

Curds and whey form at pH 4.5.

separation

curds   whey

pressed and matured

hard cheese

■ Ripening cheese

The bacteria remaining in the curds continue to work and ripen the cheese. So, the flavour of a cheese changes as it ripens. Different cheeses take different lengths of time to ripen.

We mature mild cheeses like Caerphilly for a few weeks and mature cheddars for six months. Mature cheeses have a strong taste.

3 What happens to the flavour of a cheese as it ripens?

Cheese makers produce cheeses with different tastes and textures by adding different bacteria and **moulds** to the curds.
Dairies keep special cultures of the particular microorganisms that they use.

4 Look at the pictures. Then copy and complete the table. [You do not need to know the names of these bacteria.]

Cheese	Extra microorganism used
_____ _____	_Penicillium roqueforti_ (a mould)
_____	_Penicillium camemberti_ (a _____)
Gruyère	_Propionibacterium_ (a _____)

a A bacterium called _Propionibacterium_ gives Gruyère its taste. It produces carbon dioxide that makes the holes.
b We use a mould called _Penicillium roqueforti_ to mature Blue Stilton cheese.
c We use a mould called _Penicillium camemberti_ to mature Camembert.
d Cambozola.

5 What did the cheese maker use to mature the cambozola? Explain your answer.

What you need to remember [Copy and complete using the **key words**]

More about making cheese

The starter cultures we add to warm milk to make cheese are _____ from the ones that make yoghurt. The bacteria in the cheese starter culture make curds that are more solid than the ones in yoghurt. We separate the solid _____ from the watery _____.
After separation, the bacteria slowly ripen the cheese. Sometimes we add other bacteria or _____ to produce cheeses with different colours, tastes and textures.

Industrial fermenters

Many industries use microorganisms and enzymes to manufacture their products. They are called biotechnology industries.

The photograph shows a large **fermenter** for growing a mould called *Penicillium* on a large scale. We get penicillin from this mould. We make fuels such as ethanol and biogas in a similar way.

1 What is biotechnology?

Penicillium fermenters.

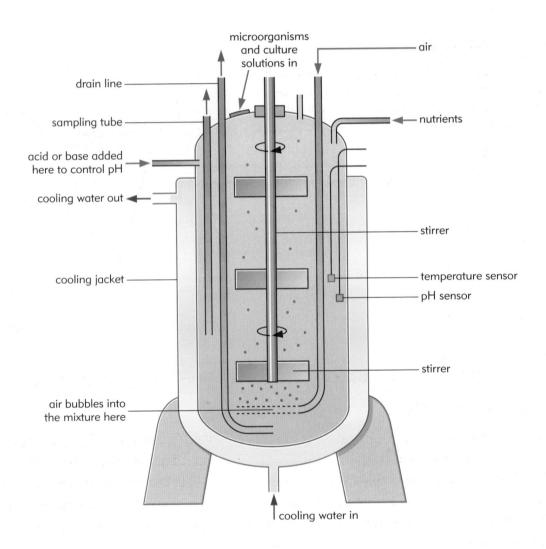

What happens inside a fermenter?

Microorganisms grow best in particular conditions. So fermenters have instruments to check automatically that conditions such as **pH** stay the same. We say that they **monitor** the conditions.

The stirrer mixes the contents of the fermenter to keep the contents and the **temperature** even. It stops the microorganisms settling to the bottom. We say that it keeps them in **suspension**.

2 Look at the diagram on page 74. Write down <u>two</u> conditions that are kept the same in this fermenter.

3 Write down <u>two</u> parts of the fermenter that help to keep the temperature constant.

4 Why does the temperature inside a fermenter tend to rise?

5 Why is air pumped into the fermenter?

■ More about penicillin

We grow *Penicillium* mould in a medium containing **sugar** and other nutrients. It uses them to feed, **grow** and **reproduce**, but it doesn't make penicillin at first. It does this only when it starts to run out of nutrients.

6 Look at the graph.

  (a) During which 24-hour period is the growth rate of *Penicillium* fastest?

  (b) After how many hours does it start to make penicillin?

  (c) Why does it start to make penicillin at this time?

7 The mould stops making penicillin after about 150 hours. Use information from the graph to suggest why this happens.

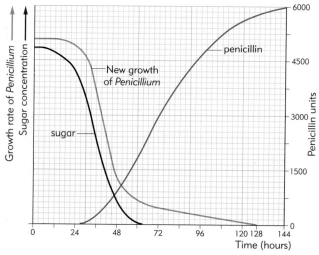

Penicillin is produced as the *Penicillium* culture runs out of sugar.

What you need to remember [Copy and complete using the **key words**]

Industrial fermenters

We can grow microorganisms on a large scale in a vessel called a _____. Instruments _____ conditions such as _____ and _____ so that they can be carefully controlled. Air is bubbled into fermenters to provide the _____ that the microorganisms need for respiration. A stirrer keeps the microorganisms in _____ and the temperature even. Microorganisms produce thermal _____ as they respire, so a water-cooled jacket removes the excess.

Penicillin is an antibiotic made by a mould called _____. We produce it on a large scale in a fermenter. The growing medium in the fermenter contains _____ and other nutrients. The mould uses up most of the nutrients to _____ and _____. Then it starts to make penicillin.

H4 **For Higher Tier students only**

Biogas

Ideas you need from *Environment*

■ Waste that comes from living things is called organic waste. Sewage is an example.

■ Methane gas is produced when microorganisms break sewage down in the absence of oxygen.

Methane is a useful fuel. The word equation for burning methane is:

methane + oxygen → carbon dioxide + water + energy

The natural gas that we burn in our homes is mainly methane. We get most of it from rocks under the North Sea. Like coal and oil, methane is a fossil fuel. It formed millions of years ago by the anaerobic decay of plant and animal remains.

We cannot make more coal and oil, but we can make more methane. We can do this on a large or a small scale. As in the past, making methane is an anaerobic fermentation process.

Anaerobic microorganisms can make methane from all sorts of materials produced by living things. We call these organic materials. The microorganisms use the carbohydrates and other nutrients in organic materials as energy sources. Many different microorganisms take part. They work faster when they are warm.

The methane made in this way is called **biogas**. We call the **fermenters** in which it is made **biogas generators**.

1 (a) What is biogas?

 (b) Why do you think it was given that name?

2 What is a biogas generator?

3 What do we call the process that breaks down materials in biogas generators?

4 Write down <u>four</u> waste materials that we can use to make biogas.

5 Write down <u>three</u> groups of people who use biogas as a fuel.

In some sewage works, methane gas is collected and used to run pumps, stirrers and even sewage works vans.

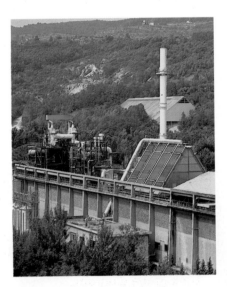

This factory makes biogas from cereal waste.

All sorts of organic wastes go into this biogas generator in an Indian village.

Biogas generator design

6 A plastic or concrete lining stops oxygen getting in and liquid getting out of a biogas generator. Write down <u>one</u> reason for:

(a) keeping oxygen out

(b) keeping liquid in.

7 Look at the diagram.
Sinking the generator in the ground like this helps to keep the contents warm.

(a) Write down the process that produces the heat inside the generator.

(b) Why does the generator produce gas more quickly when the contents are warm?

8 Some generators have stirrers run by electricity. Write down <u>one</u> advantage and <u>one</u> disadvantage of this.

9 In India, many people cook on fires of wood or dried animal dung. Dung is a valuable fertiliser, so burning it is a waste.

(a) Explain how a biogas generator in a village gives the people fuel <u>and</u> fertiliser.

(b) Explain any other benefits to the villagers of having a biogas generator.

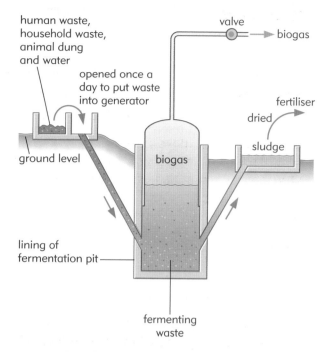

There are millions of biogas generators like this in villages in India and China.

Using your knowledge

Waste tips produce biogas too. When the gas escapes, it adds to global warming. A large tip produces enough gas to fire a power station. The gas is about 75 % methane and the rest is a poisonous, smelly mixture of carbon dioxide, ammonia and hydrogen sulphide.

Look at the diagram.

1 What do you think the power station operators have to do to the gas before they burn it to generate electricity?

2 Write down <u>two</u> economic and <u>two</u> environmental benefits of making electricity from biogas instead of fossil fuels.

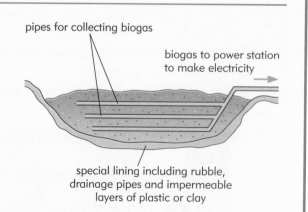

[You need to be able to (a) look at the design of a biogas generator and evaluate the advantages and disadvantages of its features, and (b) interpret economic and environmental data about biofuels such as biogas.]

H5 For Higher Tier students only

Another biofuel – ethanol

In the UK, we run our cars on petrol, diesel or methane gas. In Brazil, most people run their cars on ethanol or on gasohol. Ordinary car engines will run on gasohol. It costs a few hundred pounds to alter them to run on ethanol, but ethanol is much cheaper than petrol and gasohol. So in Brazil, they now make new cars that run on ethanol.

Brazil hasn't enough foreign currency to buy all the oil it needs to make petrol, but it does produce lots of sugar that it can use to make ethanol.

REMEMBER

Anaerobic respiration (fermentation):

$$\text{sugar} \xrightarrow{\text{yeast}} \text{ethanol} + \text{carbon dioxide} + \text{energy}$$

80% petrol — Gasohol — 20% ethanol

1 What is gasohol?

2 Write down <u>two</u> benefits to Brazilians of using ethanol as a fuel.

3 Write down the name of:

(a) the process that turns sugar into ethanol

(b) the microorganism that we use.

The mixture that comes out of the fermenter is only about 12% ethanol and does not burn.

■ Making the ethanol into a fuel

In Brazil, they burn sugar cane waste to distil the ethanol and water mixture. Distillation produces concentrated ethanol that will burn. The ethanol sold in Brazil for cars usually contains 3% of petrol to stop people drinking it.

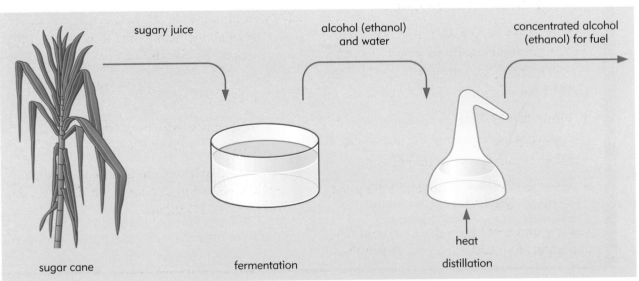

sugary juice → alcohol (ethanol) and water → concentrated alcohol (ethanol) for fuel

sugar cane   fermentation   heat   distillation

Why don't we use ethanol in cars in the UK?

We produce petrol from North Sea oil. But we also import a lot of oil. Many people think that burning the chemicals in oil is a waste. We could use them to make materials such as plastics.

Sugar cane doesn't grow in the UK. We grow beet for sugar, but we don't have enough. We could produce ethanol from other carbohydrates. This is economic only if the carbohydrates are cheap. Then we can ferment them to produce ethanol.

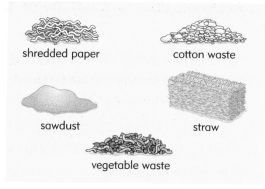

shredded paper cotton waste

sawdust straw

vegetable waste

We can use acids or enzymes to change these cheap carbohydrates into sugars. Then we can ferment the sugars and distil the ethanol just like they do in Brazil.

4 Copy and complete the flow chart.

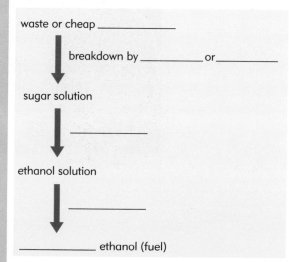

waste or cheap _____

breakdown by _____ or _____

sugar solution

_____

ethanol solution

_____

_____ ethanol (fuel)

5 Write down <u>two</u> reasons why using ethanol is not considered in the UK at present.

6 Write down <u>two</u> reasons why some people think that we should consider using ethanol.

Using your knowledge

Each year, a potato crisp factory produces millions of tonnes of starchy potato waste. It pays £350 000 in sewage charges to dispose of this waste.

The manager says that:

- they could change the starch to sugars and then produce yeast and ethanol

- they could sell the ethanol and the yeast for about £200 000 a year.

But it would cost £1.5 million to build the fermenters and £50 000 a year to run them.

1 How many years would it be before this scheme made a profit?

2 Who might want to buy the ethanol and the yeast?

3 Write down <u>three</u> benefits, economic or environmental, of the scheme.

[You need to be able to interpret economic and environmental data about biofuels such as biogas and ethanol.]

Growing microorganisms

We use lots of different microorganisms in industry. We use them to make food, fuel and medicines. We use particular microorganisms to make particular products. So they must not be **contaminated** with other microorganisms. They must be **pure** cultures. A pure culture contains only one species of microorganism.

A contaminated culture contains other species.
They may produce harmful substances.

1 We grow *Penicillium* to produce an antibiotic. Write down <u>two</u> reasons why the culture in the fermenter must be pure.

In laboratories, we can grow microorganisms on solid **agar** gel or in a liquid broth. We call these culture media. A culture medium needs to contain the **nutrients** that are suitable for the microorganism that we want to grow. The nutrients can include:

- **carbohydrate** as an energy source
- **mineral ions**
- proteins
- vitamins.

2 Look at the picture. Write down the sources of water and energy in the growing medium.

3 Is Jim's culture a pure culture? Explain your answer.

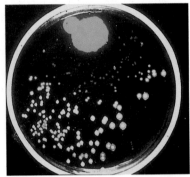

Jim grew this culture on starch agar in a Petri dish.

■ What went wrong with Jim's culture?

Microorganisms are everywhere, so it is easy to contaminate a culture. It is also easy to infect ourselves and others with a harmful species from a culture. So we need to make sure that there are no unwanted microorganisms in or on anything we use. We usually use heat treatment to kill unwanted microorganisms. This is called sterilisation.

4 Look at the photographs. Then write down <u>three</u> possible ways that Jim's culture became contaminated.

a We buy ready sterilised **Petri dishes**.

b We sterilise agar in an autoclave. It works like a pressure cooker.

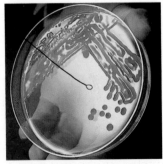

c We use **inoculating loops** to transfer microorganisms from one dish to another. We sterilise them in a flame before and after use.

■ Why was Jim still safe?

When we grow microorganisms, we always treat them as though they are dangerous. The unwanted bacteria in Jim's culture could be pathogens. They could cause disease. Jim was safe because he had sealed his culture correctly. The **adhesive tape** stops the lid coming off accidentally and letting the microorganisms out. Also, it doesn't let microorganisms in from the air to contaminate the culture.

Because he was in school, Jim incubated his culture safely at 25 °C. Most pathogens harmful to humans grow at higher temperatures than this. In industry, people **incubate** microorganisms at higher temperatures so that they grow more rapidly.

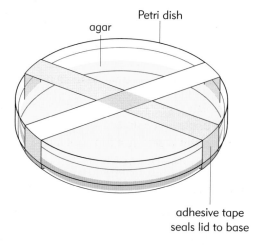

Petri dish

agar

adhesive tape
seals lid to base

5 Write down <u>two</u> safety precautions that Jim definitely took.

6 Look at the diagram.

(a) Describe how to seal a Petri dish.

(b) Explain <u>two</u> reasons for sealing it.

What you need to remember [Copy and complete using the **key words**]

Growing microorganisms

Cultures of microorganisms must be _____. They must not be _____ with unwanted microorganisms.

In laboratories, we often grow microorganisms on a medium called _____. We add to the melted agar suitable _____ for the microorganism that we want to grow.

Then we pour it into sterile Petri dishes to set. Nutrients include _____ for energy, _____ _____ and sometimes proteins and vitamins.

To grow microorganisms safely, we need to:

■ sterilise the culture medium and _____ _____ before we use them

■ sterilise in a flame the _____ _____ that we use to transfer microorganisms

■ seal Petri dish lids with _____ _____ so the lids don't come off accidentally and let microorganisms from the air contaminate the culture.

In school laboratories we _____ cultures at a maximum temperature of 25 °C.

This is because most pathogens harmful to humans grow at higher temperatures.

In industry, microorganisms are incubated at higher temperatures so that they grow more rapidly.

Moving and feeding

1 Skeletons, support and movement

Vertebrates have **internal skeletons** made of lots of bones. Bones are the rigid framework that gives you support and lets you **move**.
Muscles are attached to bones in **antagonistic** pairs. When one muscle of a pair contracts, the other **relaxes**.

2 Muscles and movement

When one muscle of an antagonistic pair **contracts**, the other muscle **relaxes**. It is only the **contracting** muscle that does the work to make a bone move. [When you are given information, you need to be able to describe the effects of muscles and bones on movement.]

3 What are movable joints like?

Strong fibres called **ligaments** hold the bones together at joints. Movable joints such as your knee move easily because:

- the ends of the bones are covered in smooth **cartilage** to stop the bones rubbing together
- a membrane secretes oily **synovial** fluid to make the cartilage slippery.

4 Is exercise good for you?

When you exercise:

- glucose and **oxygen** are supplied to your muscles at a faster rate
- heat and **carbon dioxide** are removed from your muscles at a faster rate.

Regular exercise:

- keeps the **circulation** of the blood to the heart, lungs and muscles working efficiently
- keeps muscles toned
- makes muscles **stronger** and able to work for longer
- keeps **joints** working smoothly.

But, you need to avoid sudden wrenches that can cause sprains and dislocations.

5 What makes fish good at swimming?

Fish are adapted for moving in water. They have a **streamlined** shape to reduce water resistance. There is a zig-zag arrangement of **muscles** on either side of the **backbone**. As contractions of these muscles pass along the body, they produce a **wave-like** movement. The **tail fin** has a large surface area. This fin is pushed backwards against the water, so the fish moves forwards.

6 What makes birds good at flying?

Most birds are adapted for flight.

- Their **streamlined** body shape reduces drag or **air resistance**.
- Their wings have long flight feathers so their **surface area** is large.
  The wings push down on the air to lift the bird up.
- Their **honey-combed** bones and their feathers are strong, but light in mass.

7 Feeding

Mussels feed by using their **gills** to trap **plankton**.
Beating hairs called **cilia**:

- draw a **current** of water containing the plankton through the body
- move the **trapped** plankton towards the mouth.

A mosquito feeds on **blood**.

- It has a sharp, needle-like **proboscis** to pierce the **skin** and go into a capillary.
- It secretes **saliva** into the blood to stop it clotting.
- It uses muscles in its throat to suck up the **blood**.

8 What's different about the way we feed?

Mammals use their teeth to **bite** off pieces of food. Then they **chew** it into smaller pieces before swallowing.
The **shapes** of the teeth are suited to their functions. Humans use their:

- **incisors** and canines for biting
- **molars** and pre-molars for chewing and crushing food.

[You need to be able to relate the shapes of teeth to their functions.]

9 Are all mammals' teeth the same?

A dog's jaws move up and down in a firm, **scissor-like** action.
Its **incisors** are small but provide the good grip needed to pull the meat apart.
Its sharp pointed **canines** are useful for gripping and tearing.
Its **pre-molars** and **molars** include the special, large **carnassial** teeth.
It uses these teeth to cut meat and to crush bones.
All these features are adaptations for a **carnivorous** diet.
[You need to be able to relate (a) the shapes of teeth to the jobs that they do, and (b) skulls and teeth to diet.]

Biology in action

1   What causes decay and disease?

Microorganisms that cause disease are called **pathogens**.
[You need to be able to describe Pasteur's evidence that living organisms can cause decay and disease.]

2   How do we treat diseases?

Medicines contain useful **drugs**.
Some of these drugs help to relieve **symptoms** of the disease. For example **painkillers** relieve aches and pains, but they do not kill the **pathogens** (or microorganisms) that cause the disease.
To cure the disease, the **microorganisms** (or pathogens) must be killed.
Antibiotics like penicillin kill **bacteria** but not viruses inside the body. Viruses live and reproduce inside cells. So it is hard to find drugs that kill **viruses** without damaging body tissues.

3   Do antibiotics always work?

Bacteria can develop strains that are **resistant** to antibiotics as a result of **natural selection**.
When one antibiotic no longer works against a particular **strain** of bacterium, doctors have to prescribe a different antibiotic. So to find the best antibiotic for treating a particular infection, we need to have a **range** of different antibiotics.
To slow down the rate at which bacteria become resistant, we should not **over-use** antibiotics.

4   Immunity and vaccination

You can be **vaccinated** against some diseases.
Doctors and nurses use small amounts of dead or inactive forms of a pathogen as a **vaccine**.
In a vaccine, there are proteins from the pathogen called **antigens**. These stimulate white blood cells to produce **antibodies** against these particular proteins. The antibodies can react with and destroy the antigens.
If the same pathogen gets into your body in future, your **white blood cells** can respond by making the correct antibody straight away.
So vaccination has the same effect as having the disease, without making you ill.
It makes you **immune** to the pathogen.
This is called **active** immunity because your own cells make the antibodies.

5   Vaccinations in childhood

There are vaccines to protect you against some **viral pathogens**.
Children are given the MMR **vaccine** to protect them against measles, mumps and rubella (German measles). This is **active immunity**.
If someone is exposed to a **dangerous pathogen** they need immediate protection. They are injected with the antibodies that destroy that pathogen. For example, someone bitten by a dog that may have rabies is injected with rabies **antibodies**. This is **passive** immunity.
[You need to be able to discuss the advantages and disadvantages of being vaccinated against a particular disease.]

6   How has the treatment of disease changed?

[You do not need to remember the story on pages 54 and 55. But when you are given information, you need to be able to explain how the treatment of disease has changed as a result of increased understanding of antibiotics and immunity.]

7   What happens if your kidneys fail?

If your kidneys fail, you cannot get rid of poisonous **urea** from your blood.
Some people are treated by regular **dialysis** on a machine.
In a dialysis machine, urea passes from the blood into dialysis fluid across **partially permeable membranes**.
Regular treatment is needed. After dialysis, the amount of urea starts to rise.
The next treatment restores the **concentration** of dissolved substances to normal levels.

8   Problems of kidney transplants

If a suitable donor can be found, a **diseased kidney** can be replaced with a healthy one.
This is called a kidney **transplant**. But transplanted kidneys can be **rejected** by the **immune** system of the recipient.
Some precautions to prevent rejection are to:

- match the '**tissue type**' of the donor and recipient as closely as possible

- treat the bone marrow of the recipient with **radiation** to stop white blood cell production

- keep the recipient in **sterile** conditions for some time after transplant

- treat the recipient with drugs that **suppress** the immune response.

[You need to be able to evaluate the advantages and disadvantages of treating kidney failure by dialysis or kidney transplant.]

9 Some groups of microorganisms

We use:

- bacteria to make **cheese** and **yoghurt**
- **moulds** to give blue cheeses their colour and flavour
- **yeast** to make bread and alcoholic drinks.

Moulds and yeasts are **fungi**. They have cell walls, cell membranes, cytoplasm and nuclei. Yeast is a **single-celled** organism, so each cell has one nucleus. Moulds are made of threads called **hyphae** and each hypha has many nuclei.
Moulds produce **spores** to reproduce asexually.
[You need to be able to compare the structure of moulds and yeasts with viruses and bacteria.]

10 Using yeast to make wine and beer

Yeast cells use carbohydrates as an energy source. They produce **ethanol** when they have no oxygen.

$$\text{sugar} \xrightarrow{\text{yeast}} \text{ethanol (alcohol)} + \text{carbon dioxide} + \text{some energy}$$

This is the word equation for **anaerobic** respiration in yeast. We call it **fermentation**.
In wine making, the yeast uses the natural sugars in grapes.
In brewing, the carbohydrates come from **barley** grains. Enzymes in the grains break down starch to sugars in a process called **malting**. The **sugars** are dissolved in water and fermented. Hops give the beer its **bitter** flavour.

11 Using yeast for baking

To get enough energy to grow and reproduce, yeast needs to **respire** aerobically.
But it can also respire anaerobically. This releases less energy. Both kinds of respiration release **carbon dioxide** gas.
In baking, we mix flour, sugar, **yeast** and water to make dough. Then we leave it somewhere **warm** to rise. The yeast cells respire and produce **bubbles** of carbon dioxide, so the bread rises. The bubbles **expand** when the bread is baked. This makes the bread 'light'.

12 How we make yoghurt and cheese

To make yoghurt, we add a **starter culture** of bacteria to warm milk.
The bacteria ferment the milk sugar (lactose) to produce **lactic acid**.
The lactic acid clots the **milk proteins**, solidifying the milk into yoghurt.

13 More about making cheese

The starter cultures we add to warm milk to make cheese are **different** from the ones that make yoghurt. The bacteria in the cheese starter culture make curds that are more solid than the ones in yoghurt.
We separate the solid **curds** from the watery **whey**. After separation, the bacteria slowly ripen the cheese. Sometimes we add other bacteria or **moulds** to produce cheeses with different colours, tastes and textures.

14 Industrial fermenters

We can grow microorganisms on a large scale in a vessel called a **fermenter**. Instruments **monitor** conditions such as **pH** and **temperature** so that they can be carefully controlled.
Air is bubbled into fermenters to provide the **oxygen** that the microorganisms need for respiration. A stirrer keeps the microorganisms in **suspension** and the temperature even.
Microorganisms produce thermal **energy** as they respire, so a water-cooled jacket removes the excess.
Penicillin is an antibiotic made by a mould called *Penicillium*. We produce it on a large scale in a fermenter. The growing medium in the fermenter contains **sugar** and other nutrients. The mould uses up most of the nutrients to **grow** and **reproduce**. Then it starts to make penicillin.

15 Growing microorganisms

Cultures of microorganisms must be **pure**. They must not be **contaminated** with unwanted microorganisms. In laboratories, we often grow microorganisms on a medium called **agar**. We add to the melted agar suitable **nutrients** for the microorganism that we want to grow.
Then we pour it into sterile Petri dishes to set. Nutrients include **carbohydrate** for energy, **mineral ions** and sometimes proteins and vitamins.
To grow microorganisms safely, we need to:

- sterilise the culture medium and **Petri dishes** before we use them
- sterilise in a flame the **inoculating loops** that we use to transfer microorganisms
- seal Petri dish lids with **adhesive tape** so the lids don't come off accidentally and let microorganisms from the air contaminate the culture.

In school laboratories we **incubate** cultures at a maximum temperature of 25 °C.
This is because most pathogens harmful to humans grow at higher temperatures.
In industry, microorganisms are incubated at higher temperatures so that they grow more rapidly.

Glossary/index

[Note: Concepts that are also to be found in the basic *Science Foundations: Biology* (*New Edition*) text have <u>not</u> been included unless those concepts are developed further in this text.]

A

active immunity: when your own *lymphocytes* make *antibodies* against *pathogens*; the kind of *immunity* that you get from having a disease or being vaccinated against it 51

aerofoil: the shape of a wing in section; air flows faster over the upper surface producing lift 24

agar: a gel made from seaweed used to make solid *culture media* for growing bacteria and fungi 80–81

agglutination: sticking together of red blood cells, for example when blood of different groups mixes 63

air resistance: the friction force on something moving through air; also called *drag* 23–24

anaerobic respiration: release of energy from food without the use of oxygen; *fermentation* in *yeast* is an example 66–68

antagonistic pair: a pair of muscles that work against each other; when one contracts, the other relaxes 7–9

antibiotics: chemicals produced by *moulds* that kill bacteria in your body 46–49, 54–55, 80

antibiotic resistance: when bacteria are not killed by an antibiotic; bacteria can be resistant to one or to several *antibiotics* 48–49

antibodies: chemicals made by *lymphocytes* to destroy microorganisms and other foreign bodies; also injected into the blood to provide *passive immunity* 51–53, 56–57, 60, 63

antigen: proteins on the surface of cells that the *immune* system recognises as 'foreign'; they cause the production of *antibodies* 51, 56–57, 60, 63

antiseptics: substances that slow the growth of bacteria and are safe to use on the skin 45

aphids: insects such as greenfly that feed by sucking plant sap 31

B

B-cell, B-lymphocyte: a kind of *lymphocyte* that secretes *antibodies*; some B cells are *memory cells* 56–57

biogas: a gas, mainly *methane*, that microorganisms produce when they *ferment* waste in the absence of oxygen; a useful fuel 76–77, 79

biotechnology: the use of microorganisms and enzymes in industry 74

blood group: group of people whose blood has the same *antigens* on the red cells; blood from people with the same blood group can be mixed without clumping the red cells 63

blood transfusion: blood from a donor is put into the blood circulation of a recipient; the blood must match 63

breastbone: the bone in the chest to which the ribs are attached; also called the *sternum* 27

broth: liquid *culture medium* for growing bacteria 43, 80

C

caecum: a blind-ending organ where the small and large intestines meet; where cellulose-digesting bacteria live in rabbits 38, 41

canine teeth: conical teeth between the *incisors* and *molars*; very long in *carnivores* 35–37

carnassial teeth: very large back teeth in some *carnivores* designed to cut like scissors 36

carnivore, carnivorous: flesh-eating animals 36–37

cartilage: a tissue in the skeleton; slightly compressible and smoother than bone 10, 11, 14–15

cellulose-digesting bacteria: bacteria that digest cellulose; made by microorganisms in the guts of *herbivores* 39–40

cilia: tiny hairs that move back and forth, found on the surface of some cells; they produce the current of water across mussel *gills* 28

circulate, circulation: when blood flows through the heart, arteries, capillaries and veins 12

contract, contraction: in the case of a muscle, become shorter and fatter; muscles do this to cause movement 7–9, 12, 17, 19

culture medium, media: substances like *agar* and *broth* used for growing microorganisms 80

curds: the solid part produced when bacteria turn milk sour; used to make cheese 70–73

D

dislocate, dislocation: when a bone is forced out of a *joint* 11, 13, 16–17

drag: the friction force on something moving through air; also called *air resistance* 18, 23

dialysis: separating large and small molecules using a *partially permeable membrane*, for example in a *kidney machine* 58–60, 62

dialysis fluid: the fluid used on one side of the membrane in *dialysis* 59, 62

donor: someone who donates or gives; some people donate blood or body organs 60–61, 63

E

ethanol (alcohol): a substance produced in *anaerobic respiration* by yeast; an ingredient of alcoholic drinks; also used as a fuel 66–68, 78–79

F

ferment, fermentation: breakdown of organic materials such as sugars by microorganisms such as yeast 65–67, 71, 79

fermenter: a vessel in which microorganisms are grown to make substances such as *penicillin* and *ethanol* 74–76, 79–80

fins: in a fish, they are semi-rigid parts used for steering, braking and for stability 19–21

G

gasohol: *ethanol* mixed with petrol for use as a fuel in cars 78

gills: organs for gas exchange in some animals that live in water; also used by some animals for filter feeding 28

H

herbivores: animals that are adapted to eat plants 37, 39–41

housefly: insect that feeds by sucking up liquid food through its *proboscis* 32–33

hypha, hyphae: thread-like structures that make up many fungi 64–65

I

immune, immunity: able to resist an infectious disease because you have had the disease or you have been immunised against it 50–51, 55–56

immunise, immunisation: using a *vaccine* to make your *immune* system able to resist a disease 54

incisors: sharp front teeth for biting and gripping 35–37

incubate: keep in suitable conditions for growth 81

J

Jenner, Edward: 50

joint: a place where bones meet; bones move at some joints but not at others 6, 8, 10–13, 16

K

keel: in birds it is an extension of the *breastbone* for attachment of large flight muscles 23, 27

kidney machine: another name for a *dialysis* machine: used to 'clean' the blood when kidneys fail 58, 62

Kolff, Willem: 62

L

lactic acid: a chemical produced in *anaerobic respiration* in muscles and by bacteria feeding on milk to produce yoghurt or cheese 71–72

Landsteiner, Karl: 63

Leeuwenhoek, Anton van: 42

ligament: strong fibrous tissue that hold bones together at *joints* 10–14, 15–16

Lister, Joseph: 45

lymphocytes: white blood cells 56–57

M

malaria: a disease caused by a *parasite* that lives part of its life in human red blood cells and part in a mosquito 30

measles: an infectious disease; one of the diseases that *MMR vaccine* protects against 52–53

memory cells: *B-lymphocytes* that provide *immunity* by remaining in the body when an infection is over 57

methane: the main gas in *biogas*; a biofuel 76–78

MMR: measles, mumps and rubella vaccine 52–53

molars: large teeth at the back of the jaws 35–37

Montague, Lady Mary Wortley: 50

mosquito: an insect that spreads *malaria* 29–31

mould: fungi that cause decay; some are used to make cheese, some to make *antibiotics* 64–65, 73

multiple drug resistance: when a microorganism is resistant to several different *antibiotics* 49

mumps: an infectious disease; one of the diseases that *MMR vaccine* protects against 52–53

mussel: an invertebrate that lives on rocky shores and feeds by filtering *plankton* out of the water with its *gills* 28

mutualism: a relationship between organisms of different species in which both benefit 40

O

osteoporosis: a disorder in which bones lose calcium and become brittle 15

P

painkillers: drugs such as paracetamol that relieve pain 46–47

parasite: an organism that feeds in or on the body of another living organism 30

partially permeable membrane: a membrane that allows the passage of some substances but not others; the membranes in *kidney machines* are partially permeable 59, 62

passive immunity: short-lived *immunity* to a disease when you are injected with *antibodies* 53

Pasteur, Louis: 42–45

pasteurisation: heat treatment of food or drink to kill *pathogens* without spoiling the taste 43, 70, 72

pathogens: organisms that cause disease 45–47, 51, 53, 56, 70, 81

penicillin: an antibiotic made by a *mould* called *Penicillium* 46, 73–75, 80

Penicillium: mould; we make cheese using one kind and *penicillin* from another 43, 70, 72

pentadactyl limb: a limb with five digits 26

Petri dish: a dish in which we grow microorganisms on *agar* jelly 80–81

plankton: microscopic plants and animals that live in the surface layers of water 28

preen: birds tidy and oil their feathers to keep the barbs hooked together; this keeps the surface of the flight feathers smooth 25

pre-molars: double teeth in front of the molars 35–37

proboscis: mouthparts of insects that feed by sucking or piercing and sucking 29, 32–33

R

recipient: someone who receives, for example a donated organ or blood 61, 63

reject, rejection: when the *immune* system starts to destroy a *transplanted* organ 60–61

rennet: an enzyme used in cheese-making 72

rubella: an infectious disease; one of the diseases that *MMR vaccine* protects against 52–53

rumen: a pouch between the oesophagus and the stomach of animals such as sheep and cows; *cellulose-digesting bacteria* live there 40

S

Scribner, Bolding: 62

Spallanzani, Lazzaro: 43

starter culture: a culture with microorganisms of the correct kind in the correct proportions to do a particular job 70–73

sterilise, sterilisation: killing microorganisms, often by heat treatment 59, 61, 80–81

sternum: another word for *breastbone* 27

streamlined: a shape that reduces *water* or *air resistance* 18, 23–24

swim bladder: a gas-filled bladder just under the backbone of a fish; it gives the fish buoyancy 21

synovial fluid: slippery liquid that reduces friction in a *synovial joint* 10–11

synovial joint: a movable joint that has *synovial fluid* to help the joint move easily 10–11

synovial membrane: the membrane in a joint that secretes *synovial fluid* 10–11

T

T-cell, T-lymphocyte: a *lymphocyte* that destroys cells with *antigens* on their surface 56–57

tendon: fibrous tissue that attaches muscles to bones; with tensile strength and little elasticity 17

toxins: poisons, including those that microorganisms produce 30

transplant: when an organ from a *donor* is put into the body of a *recipient* 60, 63

tuberculosis (TB): a disease of the lungs caused by bacteria 49, 54–55

U

urea: poisonous waste made when the liver breaks down excess amino acids; removed from the blood by the kidneys or by a *kidney machine* when the kidneys fail 58–59

V

vaccine, vaccination: made from dead or weakened *pathogens*; used to produce *immunity* to the pathogen 50–56

viruses: microorganisms which can only live inside cells; viruses cause diseases and *antibiotics* do not kill them 42, 46–47, 51–52, 56–57, 64

W

water resistance: the friction force on something moving through water; also called *drag* 18

whey: the liquid part produced when bacteria turn milk sour 70, 72

Y

yeast: a microorganism that carries out *anaerobic respiration* to produce *ethanol* and carbon dioxide: used in making bread and ethanol 64–69, 78–79